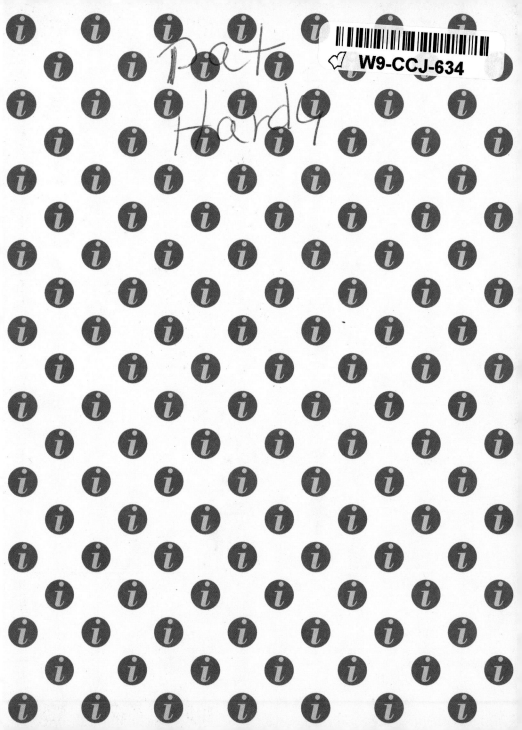

Pat
Hardy

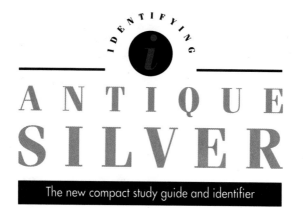

IDENTIFYING
ANTIQUE
SILVER

The new compact study guide and identifier

IDENTIFYING

ANTIQUE
SILVER

The new compact study guide and identifier

Lydia Darbyshire

CHARTWELL
BOOKS, INC.

A QUINTET BOOK

Published by Chartwell Books
A Division of Book Sales, Inc.
110 Enterprise Avenue
Secaucus, New Jersey 07094

This edition produced for sale in the U.S.A., its territories
and dependencies only.

ISBN 0-7858-0047-6

This book was designed and produced by
Quintet Publishing Limited
6 Blundell Street
London N7 9BH

Creative Director: Richard Dewing
Designer: Nicky Chapman
Project Editor: Katie Preston
Photographer: Cliff Wells

Typeset in Great Britain by
Central Southern Typesetters, Eastbourne
Manufactured in Singapore by Bright Arts Pte Ltd
Printed in Singapore by Star Standard Industries (Pte) Ltd

ACKNOWLEDGMENTS
Photographs on pages 17(b), 21(t), 24(l), 32(r,l), 38(t,b), 40(l), 54(t), 56(t), 65(b), 66(t), 74(b), 76(l) reproduced by kind permission of Sotheby's, London
Photographs on pages 14(t,b), 25(t), 31(t) © 1992 Sotheby's Inc (New York).
The Publishers would like to thank Vivienne Bryan, Joel Langford and Steven Linden of the London Silver Vaults for all their help with this project. Thank you to the members of the London Silver Vaults who kindly supplied pieces for photography: Argenteus Ltd, L. Brian, Bryan Douglas, R. Feldman Ltd, I. Franks, M. & J. Hamilton, Stephen Kalms Antiques, Langfords, Linden & Co (Antiques) Ltd, Percy's (Silver) Ltd, Rare Art, Jack Simons (Antiques) Ltd, S. & J. Stodel, William Walters Antiques Ltd, Peter K. Weiss.

CONTENTS

INTRODUCTION

Silverware in all its manifestations has proved to be one of the most popular and enduring of all the decorative arts. Although many fine pieces have been melted down, sometimes to be re-fashioned into new items or sometimes simply to realize the intrinsic value of the silver, those artefacts that have survived provide us with a glimpse of fashionable trends over the last three centuries.

The silver articles illustrated and described in this book are divided into six main groups, covering the main types of piece that collectors are likely to find. A final selection describes some miscellaneous items of domestic silverware, many of which are as keenly collected as, say, candlesticks or tankards. The pieces have been selected to cover as wide a range of makers and styles as possible, and they are, in general, the kinds of silver that collectors will encounter at auctions and through specialist dealers. Ecclesiastic silver has, therefore, not been included.

British silver is unique in that it is hallmarked with a series of punches that indicate date of manufacture, the assay office at which the piece was tested and marked, the maker and the standard of the silver used. This system of hallmarking makes British silver especially popular with collectors, and it is, therefore, well represented in the pages that follow. However, wherever possible, examples of contemporary European and American silver have been included to illustrate similarities and differences in fashion.

SILVER STANDARDS AND HALLMARKING

In its pure form silver is too soft for practical use, and it is therefore combined with very small amounts of copper. The ideal proportions were discovered to be 925 parts pure silver to 75 parts copper, and this mix has been in common use in Britain from the early 13th century until the present day, almost without interruption. It is known as sterling silver, and its use was and is rigidly and rigorously enforced by The Worshipful Company of Goldsmiths and Silversmiths, the regulating body or guild.

The system whereby marks are punched onto silver or gold items by an assay office is known as hallmarking. Its purpose is to establish the purity of the metal used, and in Britain the hallmark consists of the sterling mark (a lion passant) and other symbols to denote the place of assay, the date and the maker or makers. The testing or assaying procedure has always been applied not only to the main body of an article but also to any part, such as a handle, lid or finial, that can be detached by removing a pin or screw. Once their authenticity has been established, these parts are hallmarked as well as the main piece, although often with only the mark for sterling silver and, occasionally, the maker's mark. Individual parts, such as a removable cover, may bear the same full set of hallmarks as the main piece itself.

– BRITISH ASSAY TOWNS –

London	1716, Britannia standard
	1736, Sterling standard
	1756, Sterling standard
	1776, Sterling standard
	1796, Sterling standard
	1816, Sterling standard
	1836, Sterling standard
	1856, Sterling standard
Birmingham	1773, Sterling standard
	1849, Sterling standard
Sheffield	1824, Sterling standard
	1844, Sterling standard
Edinburgh	1780, Sterling standard
	1806, Sterling standard

In 1238 a royal ordinance decreed that wrought plate should be the same standard as the coinage – i.e., sterling – but it was not until 1300 that a compulsory mark was introduced to provide evidence of quality. In 1363 every master silversmith was required to have a personal mark, to be struck on the piece after it had been assayed. At first symbols were used for this purpose, but by the early 18th century the first two initials of the silversmith's surname were usually used. By c.1720 the initials of the first name and surname were used, and this is still customary today.

In 1477 it was decreed that London silversmiths should be collectively responsible for any failures or oversights made by the assay warden, and the silversmiths themselves introduced a mark that would enable them to identify the individual responsible. This mark was the date-letter, beginning with A in 1478 and to be changed every year thereafter. The style of the letter was to be changed after the letters had run for 20 years or so. Today date-letters run alphabetically, but in the past the system was rather haphazard.

In the early 1540s Henry VIII began to debase the coinage, and by 1544 it consisted of only half silver and half alloy. Gold and silversmiths sought to reassure their patrons of the quality of the metal they were using

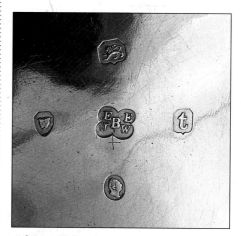

A full set of hallmarks stamped on the underside of a Victorian coffee pot. All the detachable parts of the pot are marked separately.

by introducing another mark, a complete lion passant guardant. In 1720 the use of this mark was extended to all the existing provincial English assay offices, and it was also adopted at Sheffield and Birmingham, when they opened in 1773.

From December 1784 another mark began to be applied to denote the payment of duty at 6 pence per ounce. This took the form of the sovereign's head in profile – George III was the first – and the duty was in force until 30 April 1890, when British silversmiths successfully petitioned parliament to remove the tax. Monarchs' head stamps have been used only intermittently since that time.

The system of impressing symbols into gold and silver articles is an extremely efficient method of quality control. The marks show the place of origin, the identity of the maker, the year of manufacture and the silver content of the article.

BRITANNIA STANDARD

During the English Civil War huge amounts of silverware were melted down and converted to coinage to pay the troops on both the Royalist and Parliamentarian sides, but after the Restoration (1660) the demand for domestic silver was so great that the reverse happened – coins began to be clipped or even melted down to fashion into articles. In 1697, therefore, silversmiths

– BRITISH MAKERS –

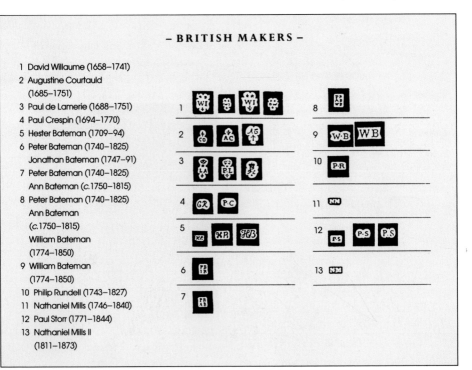

1 David Willaume (1658–1741)
2 Augustine Courtauld
(1685–1751)
3 Paul de Lamerie (1688–1751)
4 Paul Crespin (1694–1770)
5 Hester Bateman (1709–94)
6 Peter Bateman (1740–1825)
Jonathan Bateman (1747–91)
7 Peter Bateman (1740–1825)
Ann Bateman (c.1750–1815)
8 Peter Bateman (1740–1825)
Ann Bateman
(c.1750–1815)
William Bateman
(1774–1850)
9 William Bateman
(1774–1850)
10 Philip Rundell (1743–1827)
11 Nathaniel Mills (1746–1840)
12 Paul Storr (1771–1844)
13 Nathaniel Mills II
(1811–1873)

were forbidden to use sterling silver and instead had to use a metal with a higher silver content – 958 parts silver per 1,000, compared with the 925 parts per 1,000 of sterling silver – and new hallmarks were introduced to enable the system to be regulated. Britannia replaced the lion passant, and the lion's head erased (torn off at the neck) replaced the leopard's head crowned.

Britannia was the required standard between 1697 and 1720, and then silversmiths were again permitted to use sterling silver. The higher standard is still acceptable today, however, and pieces bearing the Britannia marks were not necessarily made in the late 17th or early 18th century.

AMERICAN SILVER MARKS

No government or state control was ever exercised over craftsmen in America, and purity standard of precious metals or date stamps were not required. Silversmiths in New York and Boston created their own guilds and set standards for themselves and their colleagues. Makers' names or monograms, and occasionally the place of manufacture or a number signifying the metal's purity, were the only identifying marks used.

An exception to this is silver from Baltimore, Maryland, the only city to establish an assay office, which operated between 1814 and 1830. The symbol used to indicate a high percentage of silver was a liberty

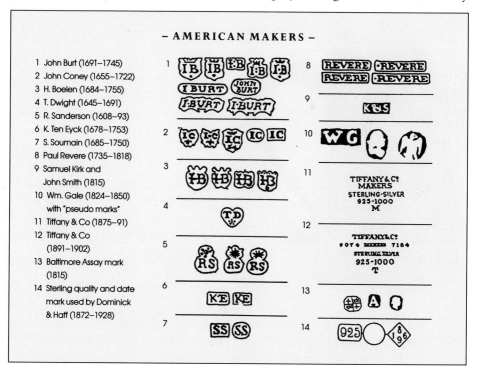

– AMERICAN MAKERS –

1 John Burt (1691–1745)
2 John Coney (1655–1722)
3 H. Boelen (1684–1755)
4 T. Dwight (1645–1691)
5 R. Sanderson (1608–93)
6 K. Ten Eyck (1678–1753)
7 S. Soumain (1685–1750)
8 Paul Revere (1735–1818)
9 Samuel Kirk and
   John Smith (1815)
10 Wm. Gale (1824–1850)
   with "pseudo marks"
11 Tiffany & Co (1875–91)
12 Tiffany & Co
   (1891–1902)
13 Baltimore Assay mark
   (1815)
14 Sterling quality and date
   mark used by Dominick
   & Haff (1872–1928)

head, the town mark, accompanied by a date letter. Before and after the existence of the assay office, Baltimore silversmiths used "11oz" or "10.15oz" to indicate a metal content of 11 ounces or 10.15 ounces of silver per 12 ounces Troy weight.

The silver content of 17th- and 18th-century pieces varied widely. If they were made from melted coins the content depended on the country of origin; if they were made from silver bullion they would be of sterling standard. After the War of Independence the mint fixed a lower standard of 892 parts per 1,000 for US coins; this was raised to 900 parts per 1,000

A tankard made between 1720 and 1730 by William Jones of Massachusetts.

in 1837 and, finally, in 1869 sterling standard came into common use and goods were stamped "sterling". From the mid-1800s until 1869 it was customary to stamp goods with an indication of quality such as "standard", "C" or "coin", "quality" or "premium".

OLD SHEFFIELD PLATE

One of the most successful ways of covering objects made of a base metal with a silver coat or "skin" was discovered *c.*1743 by Thomas Boulsover (or Bolsover, 1704–88) of Sheffield. He accidentally found that if a thin layer of silver were fused to an ingot of copper, the two metals could be rolled as one, each expanding at the same rate under pressure. Sheets of silver fused to copper could be produced in this way and then cut up to make objects. At first only one side of the copper was plated, but by the mid-1760s both sides of the ingot were silver-plated. Boulsover made small pieces – snuff boxes and livery buttons, for example – but other Sheffield and Birmingham metalworkers quickly exploited the process, and they made a wide variety of objects, including such large pieces as tureens and trays. Much old Sheffield plate is unmarked and can be dated only by comparison with hallmarked silver.

REGISTRATION MARKS

In the 1850s registration marks were introduced in Britain to record the exact date of manufacture of items of electroplate. Registration marks are not hallmarks.

CONDITION OF SILVER

The condition of any article of silver, Sheffield plate or electroplate is of paramount importance in establishing its worth, both in financial and utilitarian terms. The value of even the finest piece of antique silver will be diminished if the article has been damaged or abused, while well-cared for articles will retain their value.

Hallmarks or, in the United States, makers' marks that are so worn by use or over-polishing will cast doubt on the condition of the article and lessen its overall value. Articles made in Britain should also be appropriately marked on attached lids and handles.

A Sheffield plate dish ring dating from c.1790.

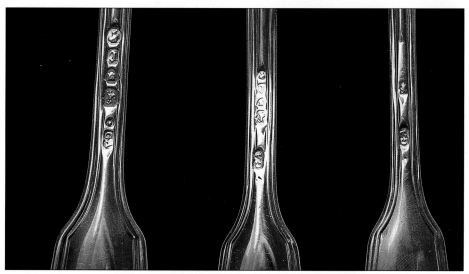

The condition of the hallmark is not only essential for identifying and accurately dating the piece, it is also a good indication of the overall condition of the article. The hallmark on the left is clear enough for the separate marks to be seen in detail; the hallmark in the centre is acceptable; the hallmark on the right, although showing the maker's mark, is so worn that it is impossible to decipher.

Throughout the 19th century early silver was often reshaped or covered with later decoration to conform to contemporary fashions. For example, the Victorian liking for naturalistic decoration led to the habit of ornamentally embossing pieces of 18th-century silver, adding scrolls, foliage, hunting scenes and sometimes even industrial scenes. Such pieces often retain their original hallmarks, and it is usually possible to sell such pieces legally. However, it is against the law to sell pieces whose original function has changed. Any added silver should also be assayed and marked.

CARING FOR SILVER

One of the pleasures of silver is its patina, the beautiful lustre that silver acquires with the passage of time and the acquisition of numerous minute scratches on its surface. Maintaining this lustre has, however, been regarded as one of the drawbacks of owning silver.

The pear-shaped tankard on the right is in its original form, but the one on the left has been changed into a hot-milk jug during the 19th century. The spout and unmarked cover have been added, ivory insulators have been cut into the handle and the whole piece has been decorated with a chased pattern of flowers and foliage.

Tarnish is a natural and inevitable process on sterling silver, Sheffield plate and electroplate, and the time taken for silver to be affected depends on the amount of moisture and pollutants in the atmosphere. Regular cleaning and polishing will help to prevent tarnish and also restore the shine. Objects that are not on permanent display or that are not used regularly can be kept in tarnish-proof bags (which are available from silversmiths and from many department stores) or storage cupboards can be lined with tarnish-preventive material. Alternatively, silver can be wrapped in acid-free tissue paper and stored in tightly closed plastic bags. Do not, however, wrap silver in plastic film, because some brands will permanently discolour the silver.

Cleaning silver, which was once carried out by the household servants under the supervision of the butler, no longer requires the application of preparations containing pumice, chalk and ammonia. Foam polishes, which have no abrasive content, are normally applied with a sponge or, if the article is pierced or highly decorated, with a nail- or toothbrush, and then rinsed off. The silver should be dried immediately after rinsing to avoid streaking. These foams have the advantages that they can give effective results with little effort and they do not cause the build-up of polish that occurs with some products. Some preparations also contain non-toxic tarnish inhibitors, which keep silver clean for up to three times longer than similar products without the inhibitors.

During the late 19th century large and highly decorated pieces of silver were sometimes coated in lacquer, a mixture of varnish or shellac dissolved in alcohol. The lacquer protected the silver from the air and retarded the process of tarnishing. Unfortunately, this lacquer tended to turn yellow with age, dulling and greying the silver beneath. Today, similar protection is in the form of cellulose or silicone coating, which gives a good finish that only requires wiping over to restore the gleam. However, applying this protective process should be carried out by a reliable firm. If it is sprayed on, any tiny pinholes that are left in the coating will allow the air to penetrate beneath and tarnish the silver, and the lacquer will have to be removed professionally. An alternative is a form of coating that can be baked on, but this is not suitable for items that have solder points or a soft base metal, which will melt during the baking process.

REPLATING

Old Sheffield plate should be replated only as a last resort. The process of electroplating, which is the only method, will give a shiny, bright and new looking appearance, changing the delicate blue lustre of sterling to the harsh white of pure silver. If more than, say, 70 per cent of the copper is showing through it is worth considering replating the item, because its value will have fallen by approximately 50 per cent. Always seek professional advice before replating an article, since good silversmiths can give an "antique" look to newly replated surfaces.

TANKARDS, GOBLETS AND JUGS

TANKARD

DATE *c.* 1710

ASSAY TOWN New York

MAKER Gerrit Onkelbag

HEIGHT 15cm (6in)

This small, tapering, cylindrical tankard has a domed lid inset with a coin within a border of leaves. The rim of the lid is similarly decorated, and the shaped front is also engraved with foliage. The thumbpiece is corkscrew-style, and the scroll handle is engraved with contemporary initials and decorated with an applied lion. The head of a putto is mounted at the terminal of the handle. The base of the tankard is ornamented with a serrated pattern of leaf tips above a wriggle-work border. The Roosevelt armorials engraved on the front within a foliate mantle with pendant swags are not contemporary with the tankard.

Gerrit Onkelbag (or Onclebagh, 1670–1732) used a close-shaped trefoil punch mark around the initials *B* above *GO*. Unlike the restrained, rather elegant work of the London-influenced silversmiths in Massachusetts, pieces made in New York tended to reflect the Dutch roots of many of the craftsmen, leavened by the French tradition of refugee Huguenots. New York tankards are often larger and heavier and more elaborately decorated and engraved than contemporary examples from Massachusetts.

TANKARD

DATE *c.* 1750

ASSAY TOWN Philadelphia

MAKER Philip Syng Jr

HEIGHT 18cm (7in)

The tapered cylindrical form of this tankard is decorated with moulded borders. It has a domed cover, and the scroll handle is applied with a beaded rattail. There is a shield-shaped terminal below a serrated border. The engraved initials *MHM* (for Mary Hollingsworth Murray) and the date, 12 November 1881, have been added later.

Philip Syng Jr (1703–89) was born in Cork, Ireland, and in 1714 he emigrated with his parents to Annapolis, Maryland, from where the family had moved to Philadelphia by 1720. His father, also Philip Syng (1670–1739), founded the family silversmithing business there, before returning to Annapolis (*c.* 1725–30). Philip Jr took over the Philadelphia business and is mostly famous for a silver standish (inkstand) made in 1752 for the assembly of Pennsylvania, which is believed to have been used by the signatories of the Declaration of Independence.

TANKARD

DATE 1773

ASSAY TOWN London

MAKER Thomas Wallis Sr

HEIGHT 19cm (7½in)

DIAMETER 12.5cm (5in)

This tapering, cylindrical, George III tankard with a simple skirt foot and domed lid is decorated only with raised bands of rib-work.

Tankards usually have scroll handles, which were cast in two halves and soldered along the back seam before being applied to the body at two points. The steam produced during the soldering process escaped through a hole cut in the underside of the handle or near the lower terminal. The lid was generally hinged above the handle, and it was fitted with a cast thumbpiece, which, during the late 18th century, was usually a simple scroll but was sometimes bifurcated or made in a corkscrew pattern. Early tankards had a skirt foot, but later examples tended to have a narrow rim foot. However, during the late 18th century there was a revival of the earlier style, as illustrated here.

The increased availability and use of glass for all manner of domestic items led to a reduction in the output of silver tankards.

TANKARD

DATE 1811

ASSAY TOWN Stavanger

MAKER Isack Andersen Feldthus

HEIGHT 19cm (7½in)

This is a traditionally shaped piece. The cylindrical, chased body rests on three ball and claw feet, and the plain hoop handle is topped by a lion thumbpiece inset with a semiprecious stone. The lid is inset with a Norwegian coin. Inside the tankard is a vertical row of equidistant pegs. The pegs indicated the amount that each person should drink as the tankard was passed around the assembled company.

Although they are more often found in Scandinavia, similar tankards were made in some parts of England, especially the east of the country – Newcastle upon Tyne, York (where John Plummer (*fl.* 1648–72) was a noted exponent of the form) and Hull, for example – from the late 16th century until the 18th century. These tankards typically have cylindrical bodies resting on three ball and claw feet or three pomegranate feet above which may be applied cast acanthus leaves. The hinged lids, which are generally almost flat, turn down vertically over the rim of the body. Sometimes the edge of the lid is decorated with a gadroon with a fluted, rosette motif in the centre. The handles are either a double scroll or a scroll widening towards the top, and they have a thumbpiece, which may be in the form of a cast, chased lion couchant or a bird.

MUG

DATE 1776

ASSAY TOWN London

MAKER John King

HEIGHT 13.5cm (5¼in)

Although a mug can be any drinking vessel with or without a handle or a lid, the word is usually used to describe vessels with one handle but no lid, unlike tankards, which generally have lids. Mugs are usually smaller than tankards.

This baluster-shaped George III mug is, as was very plain. The only decoration is provided by the double scroll handle, the upper scroll of which is embellished by a leaf. Like tankards, mugs were often decorated with coats of arms, which, especially if contemporary with the tankard, can enhance their value. Like tankards, too, mugs were usually hallmarked on the base until c.1770; thereafter the marks were generally placed on the side, near the mug's handle.

MUG

DATE 1783

ASSAY TOWN London

MAKER Walter Tweedie

HEIGHT 11.5cm (4½in)

This tapering, cylindrical, George III mug is decorated with bright cut engraving. Most mugs – if they were decorated at all – bore very simple, rather restrained ornament. They were occasionally embellished with applied strap-work or an engraved border, but crests, initials or coats of arms were usually the only decoration to be seen. During the Regency period (1811–20), however, simple, straight-sided mugs were lavishly adorned with borders of flowers and foliage.

COVERED FLAGON

DATE 1815

ASSAY TOWN London

MAKER Paul Storr

HEIGHT 16.5cm (6½in)

DIAMETER 13.5cm (5¼in)

This rare covered flagon is by one of the greatest of 19th-century English silversmiths, Paul Storr (see also page 37). The lid is decorated with a gadroon pattern, and the base is adorned with a border of anthemion and acanthus, popular motifs at this time. The thumbpiece and pouring beak are similarly ornamented, while the double scroll handle is adorned with foliage. Storr's work was invariably of the highest quality, and even insignificant pieces were well designed and executed in heavy gauge silver.

TANKARD

DATE 1868

ASSAY TOWN Birmingham

MAKER Elkington & Co.

HEIGHT 34cm (13½in)

This ivory-mounted, parcel-gilt, silver electrotype tankard is based on an original design by the French sculptor and designer of silverware August Adolphe Willms (1823–99) and chased by Léonard Morel-Ladeuil (1820–88). It is decorated in low relief over a granulated ground with entwined ivy, bands of flower heads, laurel leaves, masks and urns. The barrel is additionally inset with four oval, ivory plaques, carved with full-length allegorical figures, representing the muses of comedy, tragedy, song and dance. The plaques are below a jewelled collar embellished with the names Terpsichore, Melpomene and Thalia in dark blue enamel. The jewelled handle encloses a slithering snake, and the hinged lid is topped by an ivory infant, apparently beating time.

A version of the tankard, probably the original, was shown by Elkington & Co. at the London International Exhibition in 1862, together with a large selection of the company's recent work.

Willms was employed as head of the design department at Elkington between 1859 and his death in 1899. Morel-Ladeuil was also employed by Elkington from 1859, returning to France in 1885, but continuing to work for the company until his death in 1888.

GOBLETS

DATE 1773

ASSAY TOWN London

MAKER John Carter

HEIGHT 15cm (6in)

DIAMETER 9cm (3½in)

In the 16th and 17th centuries the use of silver to make goblets or stemmed and footed wine cups largely gave way to glass, but in the 1770s silver seems to have made something of a comeback. Goblets, such as those illustrated here, were often made in pairs and were frequently gilded inside. They were decorated with festoons and swags of fruit and flowers, which were sometimes chased, but more often bright cut engraving was used. This pair of George III goblets is decorated with contemporary armorials, and the feet are ornamented with a gadroon border.

John Carter (*fl.* 1769–77) is believed to have specialized in the making of candlesticks and salvers. He is known to have supplied candlesticks from 1769 to John Parker (*fl.* 1758–77) and to Edward Wakelin (*fl.* 1748–84), although his first mark was not entered at Goldsmiths' Hall until 1776. It is believed that Carter also worked for Robert Adam (1728–92) from time to time.

GOBLET

DATE 1791

ASSAY TOWN London

MAKER James Young

HEIGHT 16.5cm (6½in)

DIAMETER 9cm (3½in)

This plain George III goblet has a reeded foot. Between *c.* 1760 and *c.* 1820 goblets enjoyed a resurgence of popularity, having been somewhat overshadowed by the universally used mug.

The advent of new silversmithing techniques reduced the prices of goblets and made them, at least temporarily, more common. During the late 18th century the stem and base of the bowl tended to merge, and this style was often decorated with bright cut engraving and had gilt interiors. At this time the hallmarks were either placed in a straight line around the bowl or were placed in a curve around the foot.

James Young registered the mark *I·Y* in 1775.

GOBLET

DATE 1863

ASSAY TOWN London

MAKER William Smiley

HEIGHT 23cm (9in)

DIAMETER 13.5cm (5¼in)

GOBLET

DATE *c.*1890

ASSAY TOWN Not known (China)

MAKER Wang Hing

HEIGHT 20cm (8in)

DIAMETER 9.5cm (3¾in)

Fine embossing and chasing decorate this baluster-form goblet, which harks back to the thistle-shaped or campana-shaped standing cups made in the early 16th century. Victorian goblets in this style often have bold gadrooning or, as here, swirls of foliage on the base, and some had cast and applied fruiting vines on the upper part of the bowl and on the highly domed foot.

This otherwise plain goblet or wine cup is embossed around the bowl with a dragon, an auspicious motif in Chinese art, traditionally representing the season of spring and the beneficent spirit of water, as well as standing for authority, strength and wisdom. A five-clawed dragon was used to represent these qualities in the person of the Emperor, while three- or four-clawed dragons represented royal princes or important officials.

CUP AND COVER

DATE 1873

ASSAY TOWN London

MAKER Charles Stuart Harris Jr

HEIGHT 39.5cm (15½in)

The overall shape of this hand-engraved, two-handled cup is reminiscent of pieces made in the 1780s.

Charles Stuart Harris (1830–1918) is thought to have been the son of the silversmith and spoonmaker John Harris and the brother of John Robert Harris, also a silversmith and spoonmaker, and on the death of his father c.1852, Charles Stuart Harris took over the London business. Until 1860 he was in partnership with John Masters, trading as Harris & Masters. After the dissolution of the partnership, he traded as Charles Stuart Harris, using his initials, *CSH*, as his mark, until 1885, when he took over the silversmiths D.J. & C. Houle, expanding still further in 1897 when he took over the firm of Harris Bros., which had been established by two of his sons. In 1897 or 1898 the firm was renamed C.S. Harris & Sons Ltd.

CUP

DATE 1875

ASSAY TOWN Sheffield

MAKER J. Davis & Son

HEIGHT 26cm (10¼in)

This hand-chased, six-lobed Victorian cup may have been intended for use as an ornamental piece rather than as a drinking cup. The handles are formed by caryatids – cast female figures – but by this time they had become rather attenuated and rudimentary.

Today, Sheffield is one of the four assay offices outside London (the others are Birmingham, Dublin and Edinburgh). The office was instituted in 1773, when the town mark of a crown, together with the lion passant and date-letter, was established. Between 1780 and 1853 the crown mark and date-letter were usually joined in one punch. In 1975 the crown was superseded by a rose.

EWER

DATE 1702

ASSAY TOWN Dublin

MAKER Thomas Bolton

HEIGHT 25cm (10in)

The helmet-shaped body of this Queen Anne ewer is engraved with contemporary royal arms within an inscribed collar and foliate mantling. The arms are below an applied, foliate girdle and above a band of stiff leafage on a matted ground. The leaf-capped, harp-shaped handle is decorated, and the knopped and domed foot has a lobed border. The inscription reads: "Melancholy September 16 1703."

The fashion for helmet-shaped jugs or ewers, which resemble inverted helmets, was introduced into England and Ireland by the Huguenot silversmiths. The circular, spreading base of such ewers generally supports a semi-ovoid bowl, which is often divided into sections by one, sometimes two, horizontal ribs. Most of these ewers have a high pouring lip at the front and, at the opposite side, a handle. Although these handles were usually scroll-type, they were sometimes in the form of a flying scroll or in the form of an arched caryatid or mythological figure. Some examples have applied masks or other ornament below the curve of the lip.

Harp-shaped handles, a type of vertical scroll handle in the shape of an outline of a harp, were sometimes used on Irish silverware and also on some Huguenot-influenced English pieces, the style also having been brought to England and Ireland by Huguenot *émigrés.* (See also page 32.)

WINE JUGS

DATE 1900

ASSAY TOWN London

MAKER Charles Stuart Harris

HEIGHT 38cm (15in)

This pair of late Victorian silver wine jugs, in a popular design often known as the Armada pattern, is lavishly decorated with somewhat florid chasing, including grotesque masks, putti and animal heads. The design was used from *c.*1860 until the early years of the 20th century. The cartouches of these wine jugs are sometimes engraved, and the inscriptions may not be of the same date as the jugs themselves, which will diminish the pieces' value.

CLARET JUG

DATE *c.* 1870

ASSAY TOWN Paris

MAKER Jean-Claude Barreau

HEIGHT 28cm (11in)

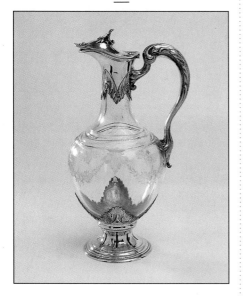

CLARET JUG

DATE 1877

ASSAY TOWN London

MAKER Edward Barnard & Sons

HEIGHT 31.5cm (12½in)

DIAMETER 15cm (6in)

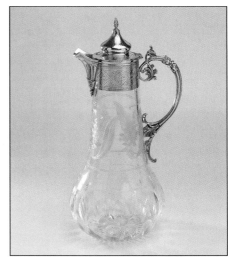

The silver mount of this French claret jug is first quality standard – 950 parts per 1,000.

A system of hallmarking has been used in France since the 14th century. The Parisian mark (a fleur-de-lys) was extended to provincial centres in 1313, and by the end of the century 186 cities were empowered to test and mark gold and silver. A system of date-lettering was also used, although this is not altogether reliable. The maker's mark surmounted by the fleur-de-lys and the assay mark were the earliest marks, with the date-letter, changing each year with the appointment of a new guildmaster (*garde de métier*), appearing later.

Gold and silver articles dating from the 18th century usually bear the mark of the *fermier*, the man who bought the right to levy duty on plate and who usually served a seven-year term. From 1765 all items of silver gilt were required to be stamped *Argent* (silver), and the discharge mark was stamped over the letter *A*.

All-silver claret jugs, sometimes called wine jugs, had first appeared in the 18th century, but it was not until the mid-19th century that silver mounts were added to glass bodies. This Victorian claret jug has a hand-engraved mount and a cut glass body.

The firm of Edward Barnard & Sons had a long, complex history, being the successors of the firm founded *c.* 1689 by Anthony Nelme and continued by Thomas, William and Henry Chawner and John Emes. By 1877 the firm was in the hands of the cousins Walter Barnard (1833–1922) and John Barnard (1835–1915), who registered the mark *WBJ* within a shield with the Goldsmiths' Hall in 1877. During the late 19th and early 20th centuries Edward Barnard & Sons made items for many of the leading retail firms, which often overstruck Barnard's marks with their own marks. It was one of the companies that enthusiastically promoted the Japanese style that became popular after the 1870s.

CLARET JUGS

DATE *c.*1895
___
ASSAY TOWN Not known (Germany)
___
MAKER Not known
___
HEIGHT 24cm (9½in)
___

These elegant German claret jugs have mounts of 800 standard silver.

In the later rococo period German silver frequently followed the lightweight excesses of porcelain design – centrepieces, for example, consisted of ornate arbours and trellises, and toilet sets were smothered in flowers, fruits and vegetables. As the rococo fell from favour in most of Germany, its place was taken by a revival in classicism. The French invasions in the early 19th century introduced new shapes and decoration in the Empire taste, and, as in Austria, this style continued until the middle years of the century, when historicism began to dominate. In northern Germany especially, English silver was popular and influential. At the end of the century German art nouveau (*Jugendstil*) came into fashion.

WATER JUG

DATE *c.*1890
___
ASSAY TOWN Not known (United States)
___
MAKER Not known
___
HEIGHT 20cm (8in)
___

This glass American water jug with silver overlay is decorated with naturalistic flowers and foliage.

Gothic and Italianate influences continued to hold sway among east coast silversmiths from the late 1850s until the 1870s. The work of New Orleans makers, on the other hand, was airy and decorative, with beading, lattice-work and gadrooning. Towards the end of the century American silversmiths were influenced by, among others, the British Arts & Crafts movement, European art nouveau and Japanese designs. Many fine individually hand-crafted pieces were made in addition to the output of the major manufacturers such as Gorham Manufacturing Co. of Providence, Rhode Island, Bailey, Banks & Biddle, Philadelphia, and Reed & Barton, of Taunton, Massachusetts.

CHOCOLATE POTS AND TEA AND COFFEE SETS

OCTAGONAL TEAPOT

DATE 1711–14

ASSAY TOWN London

MAKER Humphrey Payne

HEIGHT 22cm (8½in)

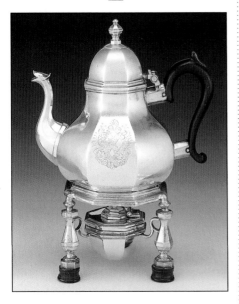

This octagonal teapot, with cast and applied spout and finial, is engraved with armorials within a formal cartouche of leafy fronds surmounted by a shell. The unmarked stand has a detachable burner resting on wooden feet and a turned wooden handle.

The earliest teapots, dating from c. 1675, were small, egg-shaped copies of Chinese forms, but by Queen Anne's reign the squat, pear-shaped (pyriform) pot with a high, domed lid and curved spout had become popular.

Humphrey Payne (fl. 1701–50) was a London silversmith, who specialized in making cups, tankards, cruets and spoons. From c. 1701 until 1720 his mark was *PA*.

BULLET TEAPOT

DATE 1729

ASSAY TOWN London

MAKER Edward Pocock

HEIGHT 9cm (3½in)

DIAMETER 10cm (4in)

This George II bullet-shaped teapot is decorated with an engraved band around the shoulder. Some examples also bear engraved armorials.

The bullet-shaped teapot is spherical in section, tapering smoothly down to the narrow rim foot and with a straight, tapering or gently curved spout and scroll handle. Most such teapots have lids that are flush with the shoulder – a drop-in lid was often used or, if there is a hinge, it will be concealed – but the example shown here has a hinge that protrudes above the shoulder.

Teapots are usually marked on the base, with a full set of marks scattered around the centre or placed in a straight line at one side, although the marks are occasionally placed on the side. Lids and handles should bear the lion passant and, often, the maker's mark. Bullet teapots commonly have wooden handles.

PYRIFORM TEAPOT

DATE *c.*1740

ASSAY TOWN New York

MAKER John Brevoort

HEIGHT 19cm (7½in)

This pear-shaped (pyriform) teapot is simply decorated with moulded borders, and the domed cover has median moulding and a raised baluster finial. The swan-neck spout is octagonal, as are the handle sockets, and the wooden handle is partially faceted to match. The mark used by John Brevoort (1715–75) was a flattened oval or trefoil punch with the initials *IBV.*

OVAL TEAPOT

DATE 1798

ASSAY TOWN London

MAKER Simon Harris

HEIGHT 18cm (7in)

LENGTH 30cm (12in)

This oval teapot has a pear wood handle and a band of reeding around the shoulder. By the 1790s teapots had become larger – reflecting the national passion for tea drinking. They were still largely flat based, and the spouts could be either straight or, as here, curved.

This simple, oval form, which was sometimes decorated with beaded borders and sometimes with bright cut engraving, remained popular for 20 to 30 years, although the flattening machinery that came to be widely used towards the end of the 18th century meant that silversmiths were able to use less silver than had been necessary for some of the smaller teapots that had been made earlier in the century.

COFFEE POT

DATE 1744

ASSAY TOWN Newcastle upon Tyne

MAKER William Beilby

HEIGHT 24cm (9½in)

DIAMETER 20cm (4in)

This coffee pot with tapering, very slightly shaped sides has a spout with shell moulding and a leaf terminal.

Newcastle enjoyed a reputation for producing fine, mostly domestic silverware, and silversmiths were working there from at least the mid-13th century, drawing inspiration from both the latest London fashions and Scandinavian designs, the latter being especially popular with those who traded along the east coast. From *c.*1658 until *c.*1672 Newcastle used a single castle as its mark. This was replaced by the three castle mark, which was used in various shields until 1883–4, when the assay office closed. From 1702 until 1721 the Britannia and lion's head erased mark, the lion passant mark (facing to the right until 1727) and the leopard's head crowned were used, the leopard losing its crown in 1846.

The Beilby family was, in fact, originally famed for making glasswares, especially for glass enamelling, and it was not until *c.*1733 that they are recorded as silversmiths. The engraver Thomas Bewick (1753–1828) was apprenticed to the "trade engraver and jeweller" Ralph Beilby in 1767. In 1738 William Beilby registered as his mark the letters *WB* with a ring above and within a rectangle.

COFFEE POT

DATE 1748

ASSAY TOWN London

MAKER Thomas Whipham

HEIGHT 23cm (9in)

Chasing or repoussé, with fluently worked scrolls and foliage, was one of the great arts of the rococo, and it was a style that was widely but often unsuccessfully imitated in the early years of the Victorian period. The chased decoration seen here is contemporary with the pot, although the lack of armorials within the cartouche detracts from the value.

This type of ornate chasing and the domed lid with acorn finial can be seen on coffee pots made in the late 1740s. The lid sometimes fits over the rim, rather than having a sleeve that fits inside it. The small hinged flap at the tip of the spout was to help conserve heat.

Thomas Whipham (*fl.*1737–75) was a London silversmith making domestic items, including sauce boats with dolphins as handles. His mark was either *T·W* (in 1737) or a cursive *TW* (in 1739) in a rectangle surmounted by a five-petalled rosette. Between 1700 and 1746 he was in partnership with William Williams, when their mark was *T·W* sandwiched between *W* and *W* to form a cross-shape; between 1757 and 1775 he was in partnership with Charles White, when their mark was *T·W* sandwiched between *C* and *W* within a circle.

COFFEE POT

DATE *c.*1750

ASSAY TOWN Dublin

MAKER Not known

HEIGHT 26.5cm (10½in)

The crest on this coffee pot is original. The swan-neck spout, which is heavily decorated near its lower end, has a hinged spout flap.

Irish goldsmiths were producing work of fine quality in the 10th century, and they are known to have been working in Dublin in at least the 13th century. However, no system of marking their artefacts seems to have been in operation before 1605, when the city council decided that every silversmith should use a personal mark and that the appropriate officials should have a stamp with a lion, harp and castle. These marks were used until 1637, when Charles I granted a royal charter, which prescribed the marker's mark and a crowned harp. In 1638 the guild instituted the use of a date-letter, and this was made obligatory in 1729, although it seems to have been rather haphazardly applied, and after *c.*1760 the date-letter was often omitted altogether. The payment after 25 March 1730 of duty on wrought plate, imposed by Walpole to fund improvements in agriculture, was indicated by a mark with a figure of Hibernia. This figure should not be confused with the Britannia mark used in England. The mark of the sovereign's head, which had been obligatory on English plate since 1 December 1784, was not applied to Irish silver until 1807; as in England, it was discontinued in 1890.

COFFEE POT

DATE early 20th century

ASSAY TOWN Vienna

MAKER Josef Hoffmann

HEIGHT 29cm (11½in)

Josef Hoffmann (1870–1956) was born in Moravia and studied architecture in Munich and in Vienna where he studied under Otto Wagner (1841–1918). After travelling in Italy, he worked in Wagner's studio until 1899. In 1897 he joined the Secession, designing the *Ver Sacrum* room at the first Secession Exhibition in 1898.

Between 1899 and 1941 Hoffmann was professor of architecture at the School of Applied Arts in Vienna. He adopted an almost totally rectilinear style – he was known as "Quadratl" ("Right-angle") Hoffmann – and the elongated abstraction of his designs owed much to Charles Rennie Mackintosh (1868–1928). He visited England with Moser, and in 1903, inspired by the example of Ashbee's Guild of Handicraft (see page 41), they founded the Wiener Werkstätte.

His preference for square decoration and chequered effects meant that his early silver wares were characterized by the smooth surfaces of the metal. In contrast, in the 1920s he turned to a curvilinear style in metalwork, and the fluted body and foot of this handsome coffee pot, together with the exotic touches of ivory, make it an especially luxurious object, perhaps more in keeping with Parisian art deco than the products of the Wiener Werkstätte.

COFFEE POT

DATE 1780

ASSAY TOWN London

MAKER Hester Bateman

HEIGHT 30cm (12in)

Silversmithing was a notable exception to the craft guilds' tradition of banning both aristocrats and women from their membership, and Hester Bateman (c.1709–93) is one of the best known names among silver collectors, especially in the United States.

On the death of her husband, John (c.1707–60), she built up his small watch and jewellery-chain business until it was one of the largest manufacturing silversmiths in London in the late 1770s. The large factory used mass-production techniques to bring the price of silverware within the reaches of the middle classes.

Her work was usually in the Adam style, although occasional pieces were not notably neoclassical. Most pieces were plain and simple, elegantly shaped and sometimes pierced, often with an engraved, bright cut band, which was often used with simple beading at the rim. Some of the articles are rather lightweight, but the spoons and forks are better quality, largely because they were still made by hand. Her mark, *HB*, first appeared in the records of the London Goldsmiths' Company in 1761, when she was working from Bunhill Row, London. From 1789 "& Co." was added to the mark, although Hester's relationship to other makers with the same surname is not altogether certain – John (1730–78), Peter (1740–1825) and Jonathan (1747–1) are assumed to have been her sons and Anne Bateman (c.1750–1815), who was in partnership with Peter, may have been Jonathan's widow. Anne's youngest son, William (1774–1850), was taken into partnership with them in 1800. The family's work extended from the late rococo period, through the neoclassical phase and into early Victorian naturalism. Some large, impressive pieces have survived, but in general the Batemans specialized in making inexpensive, simple, domestic items. This baluster-shaped coffee pot, with its restrained decoration is typical of Hester Bateman's work.

CHOCOLATE POT

DATE *c.*1718

ASSAY TOWN London

MAKER David Tanqueray

HEIGHT 22cm (8½in)

Chocolate was first drunk in England shortly after the mid-17th century, and it enjoyed its greatest popularity between *c.*1680 and 1730.

Vessels described as coffee or chocolate pots may have been used to serve both or either beverage, although strictly chocolate pots have a removable finial on the top of the lid, which exposed a small hole through which a rod – a molinet or muddler – was inserted to stir the contents before they were poured. This was so that the sediment that formed while the chocolate was infusing would be shared among the drinkers instead of being poured into one person's cup. The finials could be pulled out, twisted sideways or swung back on a hinge.

True chocolate pots also have shorter spouts or a lip at the rim; coffee pots tend to have long spouts starting from about halfway down the body. The side handle, as on the pot shown here, was popular during both the Queen Anne and George I periods.

CHOCOLATE POT

DATE 1781–7

ASSAY TOWN Limoges

MAKER Not known

HEIGHT 22cm (8½in)

This French chocolate pot on three feet, with a side wooden handle, is marked *VB*. Rather than a spout it has a short pouring lip at the rim. The three feet would not only have raised the hot base of the filled pot from the table-top, but they would also have given extra stability when the pot was stirred. For this reason, some chocolate pots have a thick foot ring instead. Projecting straight wooden handles, although often found on chocolate pots, are also sometimes found on coffee pots of the same period.

TEA AND COFFEE SET

DATE 1834

ASSAY TOWN London

MAKER Edward Farrell

HEIGHT (kettle) 35cm (13¾in)

Edward Farrell (c.1779–1850) was born in Middlesex, and his first marks were entered in 1813. It is believed that between c.1815 and the mid-1830s he was the principal supplier of Kensington Lewis (c.1790–1854), the silversmith and retailer, whose main patron was the Duke of York.

This fine quality sterling silver tea and coffee service is decorated in the style of David Teniers (1610–90), the Flemish genre artist, who specialized in peasant scenes. The pieces incorporate intricately detailed cast work as well as hand-chased scenes set in high relief. Farrell, fully exploiting the prevalent taste for naturalistic decoration, also used his chasing and modelling skills to produce enormous flagons and tankards, decorated with repoussé chasing in high relief with complicated classical scenes, in the manner of north German tankards of the 1670s. He often copied earlier styles, but is best known for somewhat florid, typically Victorian wares.

TEA AND COFFEE SET

DATE 1872

ASSAY TOWN Edinburgh

MAKER Hamilton & Inches

HEIGHT (coffee pot) 23cm (9in)

The overall shape and decoration of this sterling silver tea and coffee set clearly reveal the influence that India had on Victorian life. The signs of the zodiac are surrounded by geometric patterns and swirling foliage.

Silversmiths working in Edinburgh were associated with other "hammermen" in that city, and their records date from 1525. A deacon and other officers had been appointed by statute in 1457, and the deacon's mark and the maker's mark had to be stamped on each item. The city mark, a triple-towered castle, was added in 1485, and in 1681 a date-letter, changed each September, was introduced. At the same time the deacon's mark was replaced by the assay master's mark; this was, in turn, replaced by the thistle between 1759 and 1975, when the lion rampant mark took its place. As in England, the

sovereign's head mark was added from 1 December 1784 until 30 April 1890 to show that duty had been paid.

In 1880 Hamilton & Inches registered as their mark the italic letters *H&I* within a rectangle; in 1884 the same letters, but in Roman type, were used, also within a rectangle.

TEA AND COFFEE SET

DATE 1891–1902

ASSAY TOWN New York

MAKER Tiffany & Co.

HEIGHT (kettle) 35cm (13¾in)

LENGTH (tray) 76cm (30in) (including handles)

This complete tea and coffee set – a teapot, a coffee pot, a covered sugar bowl, a creamer, a waste bowl and a kettle on a lamp-stand – is accompanied by a matching two-handled, rectangular tray. All the pieces are decorated with a pattern of chrysanthemums.

Chrysanthemums, together with stylized bamboo stems and bulrushes, were favourite floral motifs on the Japanese-inspired tableware produced by both Tiffany and Gorham Manufacturing Company during the 1880s and 1890s, and such pieces were part of the "Japanese craze" that swept through the United States following the opening up of Japan to the West by Commodore Matthew C. Perry in 1853. Tiffany was encouraged in this by

Edward Chandler Moore (1827–91), the company's chief designer and the son of Charles Louis Tiffany's first partner, who was a keen orientalist and collector. The Centennial Exhibition helped his cause, because the display of Japanese decorative arts received widespread attention and launched the fashion for all things Japanese that was to last until the end of the century. Moore's work for Tiffany won a gold medal at the Paris Exhibition in 1878, and he had a strong influence on Louis Comfort Tiffany. (See also page 47.)

TEAPOT

DATE 1881

ASSAY TOWN possibly Birmingham

MAKER Christopher Dresser

LENGTH 25cm (10in) (including handle)

After studying at the School of Design in London, Christopher Dresser (1834–1904) began his career as a teacher of botany. He had been greatly influenced by the teachings of Owen Jones (1809–74), a close colleague of Henry Cole (1808–82), who sought to formulate rules governing design that would make it an expression of the needs and sentiments of the age. Jones's ideas were based on studies of the structure of natural forms and of past styles, while emphasizing their underlying principles rather than their results. Dresser went further than Jones, his analysis of the geometry and structural principles of natural forms leading him to reject representational and stylistic solutions. Among his most outstanding achievements was a series of metalware designs by James Dixon & Son of Sheffield and Hukin & Heath and

Elkington & Co., both of Birmingham.

His elegant, geometric forms are characterized by simplicity based on an analysis of function, and they pay attention to ease of manufacture and use. He derived aesthetic quality from enhancing the materials used, and he always stressed economy of materials to reduce costs so that, as he stated, the products might not be "beyond the reach of those who might otherwise enjoy them". Although few in number, the metal objects designed by Dr Dresser, such as this jaunty wood and silver teapot, were noted not only for their simplicity but also for their proto-modernity.

COVERED JUG

DATE 1702

ASSAY TOWN Dublin

MAKER Thomas Bolton

HEIGHT 30cm (12in)

This covered jug, dating from the time of Queen Anne (1702–14), is engraved with contemporary royal armorials. The fluted spout is decorated with leaves, and the scroll handle has a quatrefoil terminal. The girdle is applied, and the body is decorated with stiff foliage on a matted ground. The borders are lobed. The slightly domed cover is topped with a baluster vase finial and a scroll thumbpiece.

Thomas Bolton (*fl.* 1686–1702), who worked in Dublin, is regarded by many as the finest silversmith working in Ireland at the turn of the 17th century. At this period Irish silversmiths tended to use designs conforming to the styles inaugurated in London, possibly because they relied on the patronage of wealthy English landowners, who owned vast estates in Ireland. Bolton, however, would extend the basic forms in new ways. Bolton's mark (registered in 1694) was the initials *TB* within a shield-shaped punch. (See also page 21.)

HOT-MILK JUG

DATE 1717

ASSAY TOWN London

MAKER Richard Bayley

HEIGHT 15cm (6in)

The octagonal baluster body of this hot-milk jug, which rests on a stepped, moulded foot, is engraved with armorials below the short spout. The domed lid is topped with a finial that echoes the shape of the body.

At first tea was drunk without milk, but by the early 18th century it had become customary to take tea with milk or cream, which was generally warmed and served in a small, lidded pot. Such jugs were almost entirely superseded by cream or milk jugs by the early 1730s, and the few later covered jugs that were made generally resemble the style of the unlidded kind.

Such jugs are sometimes known as hot-water jugs or shaving jugs.

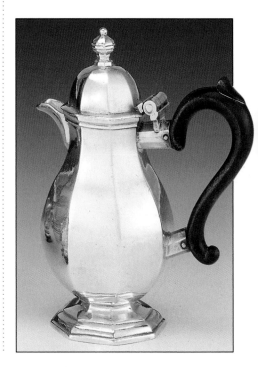

TEA KETTLE

DATE 1868

ASSAY TOWN Birmingham

MAKER Jonas and George Bowan

HEIGHT 43cm (17in)

DIAMETER 20cm (8in)

This Victorian tea kettle on a stand with a burner has hand-chased decoration of flowers and foliage. It has the typical floral and foliate chasing of Victorian designs.

Although it is not known exactly when silversmithing activities began in and around Birmingham, they were certainly well established by 1773, when a petition was presented to Parliament on behalf of the town's plate workers requesting permission to establish an assay office. Birmingham-made articles had to be sent to Chester or London, causing delay, inconvenience and expense. The proposal was resisted by the Goldsmiths' Company of London, but the petition was eventually accepted and Birmingham was appointed as an assay town. A company, the Guardians of the Standard of Wrought Plate in Birmingham, was established and given jurisdiction over all silversmithing in the town itself and within 30 miles. The mark chosen was an anchor, a symbol that is still used.

ARGYLL

DATE 1795

ASSAY TOWN London

MAKER Peter Podio

HEIGHT 17cm (6¾in)

DIAMETER 10cm (4in)

Argylls (or argyles), which are found in silver and in Sheffield plate, were made between c.1760 and c.1820. They are named, it is said, after the 4th Duke of Argyll, who designed the container to keep gravy hot. They are usually vase- or baluster-shaped, although some early examples, especially those of Sheffield plate, are of a tapering, straight-sided design. They have a handle and a spout, not unlike a coffee pot, and usually curved. The gravy was kept warm either by a hot-water jacket around the outside, or by an inner lining or central horizontal compartment for hot water, or (as here) by a heated iron billet or, possibly, hot charcoal in a cylindrical sleeve. Argylls that operated by means of an inner lining to contain hot water may have external filling points – such as in the top of the handle or opposite the spout.

Argylls were also made in pottery – Wedgwood's 1774 creamware catalogue includes an example – and delftware versions are also known. They appear to have been made only in England.

BOWLS, DISHES, CENTREPIECES AND PLATES

TABLE BASKET

DATE 1772

ASSAY TOWN London

MAKER William Plummer

DIMENSIONS 33 x 26cm (13 x 10¼in)

William Plummer (*fl.*1755–91) specialized in making pierced baskets for cakes, sugar and sweetmeats and cream pails. He used the technique of saw cutting – using a piercing saw to cut irregular and decorative holes.

Table baskets, which are often described as bread baskets or cake baskets – the name table basket occurred in a royal inventory of 1725 – were made in the late 16th century, but examples from before the early 18th century are rare. All have solid bases to prevent crumbs falling through. Those dating from the reign of Queen Anne (1702–14) were either oval or circular, and the sides, which were usually pierced with scale or lattice designs, widened from base to rim. They often had heavily moulded edges and handles.

In the 1760s and 1770s alternate pierced panels of the kind seen here, often edged with beaded flutes, became common, and the foot was of the pierced rim style. Modified versions of the pierced sheet metal type baskets continued to be made until the early 19th century, after which they were rarely made.

TABLE BASKET

DATE 1787

ASSAY TOWN London

MAKER Not known

DIMENSIONS 35.5 x 25cm (14 x 10in)

This table basket bears the initials *IH*. During the 1780s baskets became shallower, more flared and of a more pronounced oval shape. The spreading foot and rim of this George III basket are pierced with slats and an intricate geometric decoration, although bright cut engraving was also widely used, and the reeded swing handle, which is separately hallmarked, is hinged.

At this time, when silver was extremely costly and the duty payable on silver articles was high, makers strove to find designs that used the least possible amount of silver.

The handle of a table basket should bear a lion passant mark, although some examples made before 1784 do not have this mark. Soup tureen liners were sometimes converted into table baskets, and when this has happened the mark will appear distorted.

TABLE BASKET

DATE 1838

ASSAY TOWN London

MAKER Edward Barnard & Sons

HEIGHT 12.5cm (5in)

DIAMETER 33cm (13in)

In the 1820s and 1830s there was a revival of heavy, rococo-style baskets. This circular example is deeper than those seen in the late 18th century. It has a wavy rim and floridly embossed and chased floral panels. The spreading foot, in contrast, is comparatively plain.

The firm of Barnard dated back to Anthony Nelme, who was working in the 17th century. In the 1830s the firm was in the hands of Edward Barnard Sr (1767—1855), who took his sons Edward Jr (1796—1867), John (1797—1879) and William (1801—48) into partnership with him, naming the firm Edward Barnard & Sons and, later, W.J. & W. Barnard. It worked throughout the 1800s to the 1900s in London, making a range of widely available

articles, especially tea and coffee services. The silverware was consistently good, many articles combining naturalistic flower forms with cast cherubs and foliage.

MEAT PLATE

DATE 1824

ASSAY TOWN London

MAKER William Eley Jr

DIMENSIONS 44 x 57cm (17½ x 22½in)

This heavy meat plate – it weighs 3.68kg (130oz) – is decorated with a gadroon and shell border.

Most early meat plates – those made before *c.* 1830 – were marked on the outer raised rim between the inner border (the bouge) and the outer border. Later examples were marked in exactly the same place, but on the underside of the dish.

In 1795 Eley registered the mark *WE* within an oval; in 1825 his mark was a cursive *WE* within an oval.

SAUCE BOATS

DATE 1742

ASSAY TOWN London

MAKER John Cafe

HEIGHT 11.5cm (4½in)

LENGTH 20.5cm (8¼in)

Among the new tablewares that appeared in the first decades of the 18th century were sauce boats. The earliest known examples date from 1717 – they are oval with slightly wavy rims and with a scroll handle on either side and a lip at either end. In the late 1720s, however, a vessel with a handle at one end and a pouring lip at the opposite end began to be more often seen. These were generally made in pairs, and they were usually fairly plain. During the 1740s decoration was confined to the feet and to the cast, scroll or flying scroll handle.

These George II sauce boats are heavy – weighing 0.79kg (28oz) – and they have the typical, leaf-capped flying scroll handle and rather plain, applied shell feet.

John Cafe (*fl.* 1740–57) is best known as a maker of fine candlesticks, chambersticks and snuffers. In 1742 his mark was *I.C.* within an oval. His brother, William (*fl.* 1757–*c.* 75), took over his business in 1757, using as a mark (registered in 1758) the gothic letters *WC* under a rosette over a trefoil.

SAUCE TUREENS

DATE 1807

ASSAY TOWN London

MAKER Robert and Samuel Hennell

HEIGHT 15cm (6in)

LENGTH 22cm (8½in)

Sauce tureens, such as these oblong, fluted examples, offered an alternative to sauce boats for the serving of sauces, and they seem to have been first made in the 1760s. They were often made *en suite* with soup tureens, of which they were sometimes smaller versions, and they nearly always have a cover, sometimes (although not in this instance) with a small cut-out segment to accommodate the handle of a ladle. They are rarely found in silver after the 1830s, the cheapness and practicality of porcelain making silver dinner services obsolete.

Robert Hennell (1741–1811) was one of the leading exponents of the neoclassical revival in Britain during the late 18th century, and his work is typical of the period in its use of classical motifs for decoration. Five generations of Hennells were London silversmiths. Robert's father, David (1712–85) started the business, and his sons, David Jr (1767–*c.*1829) and Samuel (1778–1837) were, at various times, in partnership with him. David Sr's great-great-grandsons Robert (1826–91) and James Barclay (1828–99) continued the family firm, until James Barclay's retirement in 1887, when it was sold to Holland, Aldwinckle & Slater.

In 1802 Robert and Samuel Hennell registered the mark *R·H* above *S·H* in a square.

Soup Tureen

DATE 1798

ASSAY TOWN London

MAKER Paul Storr

HEIGHT 33cm (13in)

WIDTH 40cm (16in) including handles

DEPTH 29cm (11½in)

This elegant soup tureen bears the engraved arms of the Buller family, whose motto translates as "The eagle does not catch flies".

The principal British silversmith of the Regency period and regarded by some writers as the greatest silversmith of the 19th century, Paul Storr (1771–1844) was apprenticed in 1785 to the Swedish-born silversmith Andrew Fogelberg (c.1732–1815), who had settled in London in the early 1760s and who was one of the leading exponents of the neoclassical style. Storr first registered his maker's mark at the Goldsmiths' Hall in 1792, when he was in partnership with William Frisbee (or Frisby). The partnership was short-lived, however, and Storr quickly joined Rundell & Bridge, a firm with retail premises in Ludgate Hill in London. Rundell & Bridge had been established in 1772, when Philip Rundell went into partnership with William Pickett, whom Rundell bought out in 1785. Rundell then entered into a partnership with John Bridge, and among the silversmiths employed by them were Digby Scott (fl.1802–7) and Benjamin Smith (1764–1823).

Between 1803 and 1819 Storr was largely occupied with commissions for the Prince Regent, not only as a craftsman but also as a designer, although some of the designs he executed were by John Flaxman (1755–1826).

Storr's work exemplifies the Regency style: it is largely decorated with classical motifs based on those of Imperial Rome, but includes occasional references to Egyptian subjects, inspired by Napoleon's campaign in that country and Nelson's victory at the Battle of the Nile (1798). In 1820 Storr left Rundell, Bridge & Rundell and in 1822 he entered into partnership with John Mortimer under the style Storr & Mortimer, and their joint mark was registered at the Goldsmiths' Hall in 1821. Storr retired from active work in 1839, dying five years later in comparative poverty.

MONTEITH

DATE 1705

ASSAY TOWN London

MAKER Anthony Nelme

DIAMETER 33.5cm (13¼in)

Monteiths are large, circular or oval bowls, not unlike punch bowls, but they have scalloped rims, sometimes vertical, sometimes curved outwards, into which the feet of between six and eight wine glasses could be slotted so that the bowls could be cooled in iced water. They were first made in the 1680s, but in the 1690s they began to be made with detachable rims, which meant that they could do double-duty as punch bowls.

This Queen Anne monteith stands on a moulded, circular base. The bowl is simply decorated with applied scrolled cartouches in relief, which are engraved with a coat of arms on one side and a crest on the other. Also applied are the two mask and drop ring handles. The shaped and everted detachable lip is decorated with cast strap-work and husks.

Anthony Nelme (fl. 1650–1723) was one of the greatest English silversmiths. His well-designed and beautifully made work ranged from simple cups to massive display pieces, and he is said to have been the first silversmith in England to make a soup tureen. His son Francis (fl. 1719–39) succeeded him in 1723.

MONTEITH

DATE 1708

ASSAY TOWN Dublin

MAKER Joseph Walker

DIAMETER 34cm (13½in)

This Irish monteith has a detachable rim, which is boldly scalloped with a border of shells and scrolls, and it has applied, lion mask, drop ring handles.

Early examples of monteiths are without handles; some have had handles added at a later date. One or two gold monteiths are known, and some were made of delftware in England in the late 18th century and, later, of creamware and porcelain. A few glass examples have also survived. Silver monteiths continued to be made until the 1790s, and some were made of Sheffield plate. They are, it is said, named after a Scotsman, called Monteith, who used to wear a cloak with a scalloped edge.

In 1701 Joseph Walker registered his mark as a cursive JW within a shield.

FOOTED SALVER

DATE 1768

ASSAY TOWN Dublin

MAKER William Bond

DIAMETER 28cm (11in)

Another mid-17th century innovation to the English home was the footed salver, which was defined by Thomas Blount in 1661 as "a new fashioned peece of wrought silver plate, broad and flat, with a foot underneath . . . used in giving beer or other liquid things to save the Carpit [i.e., tablecloth] or the Cloathes from drops". Examples dating from before the reign of George I (1714–27) are rarely found, however.

These are most often plain pieces, except for engraved armorials in the centre, although some bear quite elaborate chased ornamentation in the chinoiserie style while others were engraved with designs of foliage and flowers. They generally have a single, central foot (which may be unscrewable), although a few are found with three or four small scroll feet.

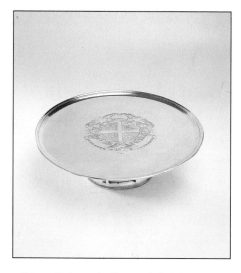

Salvers, like trays, should carry a full set of marks, which are normally in a straight line either on the top surface or the underside. In 1792 William Bond's mark was a cursive *W·B* within a rectangle.

TRAY

DATE 1865

ASSAY TOWN London

MAKER Edward Barnard & Sons

WIDTH 51cm (20in)

LENGTH 62cm (24½in) (excluding handles)

Trays did not begin to be made until the late 18th century; before that time oblong salvers were made and may have served a similar purpose. The word "tray" should strictly be applied only to pieces with two handles and no foot or feet to rest it on.

The surface of this sterling silver tray is hand engraved and bears a later (1900) presentation inscription. In the 1860s the style of the 1780s and 1790s made a reappearance, although the beaded borders, as seen here, tended to be rather bolder and the bright cut engraving less formal. Trays were often made *en suite* with tea and coffee sets and had to be large enough to accommodate all the pieces of the service.

By 1865 the firm of Edward Barnard & Sons was represented by the brothers Edward (1826–76) and Walter (1833–1922) and their cousin John (1835–1915). (See also pages 22 and 35.)

CENTREPIECE

DATE 1862

ASSAY TOWN London

MAKER Robert Garrard for R. & S. Garrard & Co.

HEIGHT 43cm (17in)

This is one of a set of three heavily cast and chased silver and coloured glass centrepieces made for the royal palace at Alexandria, Egypt. The shaped, tri-form base of each has webbed, shell-like dish-holders between bold, leafy and scrolling supports, and there are three more small dish-holders above. The central spires are formed by a twisting baluster, decorated with foliage and berried fronds, and the finials of floral clusters rest on a leafy platform.

The firm of R. & S. Garrard & Co. was founded in 1722 by the silversmith George Wickes (1698–1761), who entered into partnership with Edward Wakelin (fl. 1748–84) in 1747. The firm operated with various partners and under various names – Craig & Wickes, George Wickes, Wickes & Netherton, Parker & Wakelin, Wakelin & Taylor and Wakelin & Garrard – until 1802 when Robert Garrard Sr (1758–1818) became a partner in the firm, which became known as Robert Garrard. On their father's death Robert Jr (1793–1881) and his brothers James and Sebastian formed the firm of R. J. & S. Garrard. James Garrard retired c. 1835, and the firm became R. & S. Garrard, trading under that name until 1843, when it became R. & S. Garrard & Co.

CENTREPIECE

DATE 1876

ASSAY TOWN London

MAKER Stephen Smith

HEIGHT 63.5cm (25in) (including plateau)

DIAMETER (plateau) 45.5cm (18in)

Originally centrepieces, which were, it is assumed, designed to hold fruit or sweetmeats, consisted of a large, central silver basket surrounded by between four and six smaller silver baskets or dishes. At the beginning of the 19th century cut glass dishes began to be used together with the silver framework. This elaborate silver Victorian centrepiece and mirror plateau with cut glass dishes also incorporates three flower vases.

Mirror plateaux were used to give added brilliance and sparkle to centrepieces. Some large versions even ran the whole length of the table, being made in sections so that they could be adjusted as necessary, but most were formed from a single piece of mirror glass set in a circular, oblong or round frame and used as a support for a centrepiece or dessert stand.

Working in London, Stephen (or Steven) Smith (fl. 1850–86) made a variety of wares, including claret jugs and wine cups, that are widely available today. In 1865 he registered the mark S.S within an oval, changing this to S.S., also within an oval, in 1878.

CENTREPIECE

DATE 1911

ASSAY TOWN Birmingham

MAKER A. Edward Jones

HEIGHT 16.5cm (6½in)

DIAMETER 20cm (8in)

A. Edward Jones, who was a Birmingham designer and the son of a blacksmith, extended the family business to include silversmithing, and from 1902 the firm produced silver articles, many of which were similar in style to that of the Birmingham Guild of Handicraft, some of whose members, including Arthur Gaskin (1862–1928) and his wife, Georgina Cave France (1868–1934), may have supplied designs. Much of Jones's work was set with turquoise, and he sometimes produced silver mounts for pieces made at the Ruskin Pottery of his friend William Howson Taylor.

The Guild of Handicraft was founded by Charles Robert Ashbee (1863–1942) in 1888. He regarded silverware "as the most degraded of all English crafts" and wanted to reverse that situation. Although he intended the Guild to promote all aspects of design, it achieved recognition largely through its metalwork and jewellery. In 1902 Ashbee moved the Guild from the East End of London to Gloucestershire, but the difficulties continued, and it was voluntarily wound up in 1908. The Guild's mark, registered in 1900, was *G of H Ltd* (with the "of" contained within the bowl of the "G") within a rectangle with canted corners.

The Birmingham Guild of Handicraft was founded *c.*1890 by Arthur Stansfield Dixon and members of an evening class that he ran, and it produced comparatively large quantities of silverware as well as printing its own magazine, *The Quest*. In 1895 the Guild became a limited company, and it later moved from its original premises in Kyrle Hall to workshops designed by Dixon in Great Charles Street, Birmingham. The Guild's silverware, both domestic and ecclesiastical, is characterized by its clean lines and lack of ornamentation. Dixon was a friend of William Morris and arranged for the Guild's work to be sold at Morris & Co. in London.

BOWL

DATE 1892

ASSAY TOWN London

MAKER John Newton Mappin

DIAMETER 30cm (12in)

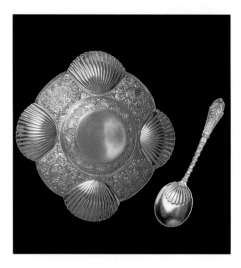

This silver gilt fruit serving bowl, with its scallop shell motif, scrolling and foliage, reveals a rococo influence, although the matching spoon has a clearly visible Egyptian motif.

The long-established London firm of silversmiths and retailers was founded *c.*1774 by Jonathan Mappin (*fl.*1774–97). The business prospered, and by 1849 several shops had been opened and the firm, now run by the great-grandsons of Jonathan, was known as Mappin Brothers. In 1864 John Newton Mappin (d.1913), who, after disagreements with his brothers, had run his own cutlery and electroplating business since 1859, took his brother-in-law, George Webb, into partnership, and although Webb died *c.*1880 the firm's name remained Mappin & Webb until 1989, when it became a limited company. In 1903 Mappin & Webb bought out Mappin Brothers. In 1889 Mappin & Webb used the mark *MN WB* above &, all within a shield-shaped punch; in 1898 the same letters but in a rectangle were used.

SALVER

DATE 1899

ASSAY TOWN London

MAKER Gilbert Leigh Marks

DIAMETER 23cm (9in)

Gilbert Leigh Marks (1861–1905) was one of the earliest Arts & Crafts silversmiths in Britain. Between 1878 and 1885 he worked in London for Johnson, Walder & Tolhurst, a firm of manufacturing silversmiths, leaving to join the firm of Masurel & Fils in London before establishing his own workshop in 1888, from where he worked in both silver and pewter. Although he carried out every aspect of the work by hand, the objects he produced look so professional that they almost disqualify themselves from being described as inspired by the ideals of the Arts & Crafts movement.

This signed, solid silver salver is typical of Marks's work, which was usually decorated with beautifully executed repoussé motifs, although they are often more reminiscent of the precise and realistic work of industrial silversmiths than of the fantastic designs favoured by the Guild of Handicraft. In 1896 Marks registered as his mark the cursive letters *GM* contained within a rectangle with canted corners.

BOWLS

DATE 1923

ASSAY TOWN Birmingham

MAKER Hukin & Heath

DIAMETER (large bowl) 30cm (12in)

During the 1920s and 1930s ivory and silver were a popular combination, and the ivory handles on this sterling silver fruit bowl and two side dishes are typical of the period.

The mark of Hukin & Heath, which was founded *c.*1855 by Jonathan Wilson Hukin and John Thomas Heath, was registered at the Birmingham Assay Office in November 1875. The firm bought designs from Christopher Dresser after his 1877 visit to Japan and made several designs in the Japanese style; Dresser, in fact, became the company's art director in 1879. One of the firm's specialities was the decoration of glass objects with silver mounts. The firm closed in 1953.

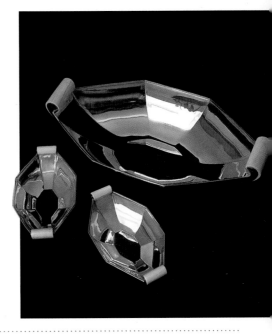

BOWL

DATE 1933

ASSAY TOWN Overmarked in London

MAKER Georg Jensen

DIAMETER 16.5cm (6½in)

HEIGHT 6.5cm (2½in)

The most famous of Scandinavian silversmiths, Georg Arthur Jensen (1866–1935) was born at Raadvad near Copenhagen. From 1880 he worked as a goldsmith in Copenhagen, gradually turning to silver work. Between 1887 and 1892 he studied sculpture at the Copenhagen Academy, where he came under the influence of C. C. Peters (1822–99), who had designed neoclassical metalwork and ceramics. From *c.*1895 Jensen designed and made sculptural ceramics, some of which were shown at the Paris Exhibition in 1900. Jensen travelled in France and Italy, becoming increasingly interested in jewellery and silver. He opened his first shop in 1904 and soon had branches in Paris, London and New York.

After a brief flirtation with art nouveau, Jensen's designs were simple, rather stumpy forms decorated with concentrated ornaments, often fruit or flowers and often restricted to features such as knobs, feet or handles. From 1907 the painter John Rohde (1856–1935) was a close collaborator and was responsible for many of the strikingly simple designs, but Jensen also employed several other artists, notably Henning Keppel, Arno Malinowski, Harald Nielsen from 1909 and Sigvard Bernadotte (the son of the King of Sweden) in the 1930s. The workshops made a wide variety of other items, tea and coffee sets, candlesticks, cocktail shakers, tureens and cigar boxes.

FLATWARE, CRUETS AND CASTERS

MARROW SCOOPS

DATE 1799

ASSAY TOWN London

MAKER William Eley and William Fearn

LENGTH 15cm (6in)

These long, thin implements were used to extract the marrow from beef bones. One end was channelled into a trough-shape to form a long, narrow scoop, but on some examples both ends are channelled but to two widths to fit bones of different sizes. They superseded marrow spoons, which have a conventional bowl at one end with the handle channelled in the form of a long, narrow scoop. Marrow scoops formed part of dinner services between c.1700 to c.1900, and they were made in great quantities in the 18th century.

APOSTLE SPOON

DATE c.1630

ASSAY TOWN Norwich

MAKER Not known

LENGTH 18.5cm (7¼in)

Spoons with finials representing the apostles were among the most popular of medieval and 16th-century spoons. Complete sets of 13 spoons are extremely rare. The bowls are fig-shaped. In most London-made examples the finials are soldered into a V-shaped joint in the tapering, hexagonal stem. In provincial spoons the finial is affixed by means of a lap joint, and the seam should be visible across the back of the shaft and down the sides of the stem. The town mark was placed in the bowl near the stem, and the maker's mark (if present) and date-letter were struck near the base of the stem. Generally the apostle carries an identifying device or symbol – St Andrew, for example, carries a saltire cross while St Peter carries a key – and the terminal disc or nimbus could be either in the form of a spoked wheel or cast with the holy dove.

The spoon illustrated is a rare example of provincial work. Norwich was one of seven provincial centres – York, Newcastle upon Tyne, Lincoln, Bristol, Salisbury and Coventry were the others – permitted in 1423 to adopt their own "touches". This town mark was the city's arms – a castle with a lion beneath.

CADDY SPOON

DATE 1858

ASSAY TOWN Birmingham

MAKER George Unite

LENGTH 11cm (4½in)

This Birmingham-made caddy spoon has an open-work, vine pattern handle and a gilded bowl. The growth of the Birmingham "toy" (smallwares) trade and the development of the tea caddy with two compartments led to the popularity of small, shell-shaped caddy spoons, which could be kept inside the caddy.

George Richard Unite was apprenticed to Joseph Willmore, the Birmingham silversmith, in 1810 and was recorded as a silversmith in London in 1852, when he traded from an address also used by Willmore and by Nathaniel Mills & Sons. In 1854 he was operating from Caroline Street, Birmingham, as George Unite, manufacturing silversmith. His mark was *GU* in an octagonal lozenge. Seven years later he entered his mark at the Sheffield Assay Office. He manufactured a wide range of items, including flatware, fish and cake slices, salt cellars, fruit spoons, napkin rings, cups of various kinds, cigar and cigarette cases, snuff boxes, card cases, bells and inkstands.

SUGAR SIFTER

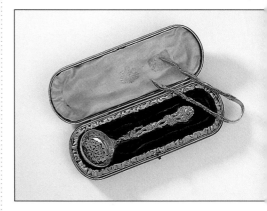

DATE 1862

ASSAY TOWN London

MAKER Francis Higgins & Sons

LENGTH 16.5cm (6½in)

By the 1750s the custom of taking sugar with tea was firmly established, and this Dutch-style, silver gilt sugar sifter spoon and accompanying tongs, which are in their original case, reflect this habit.

The design of the earliest sugar tongs seems to have been based on the steel nippers used in the kitchen to cut up loaf sugar. The scissor-type tong, about 10cm (4in) long and with looped bows, scroll shanks and shell grips, appeared *c.*1720 and was widely made between 1740 and 1760. By 1760, however, the U-shaped, springy pattern had emerged. At first they were often cast and pierced; later plain or shaped blades with spoon-like scoops were usual, the sides often decorated with bright cut engraving, with stamped shell motifs or with thread, beaded or feather-edge patterning in the style of contemporary flatware. The large sugar bowls of Victorian tea services led to the introduction of larger tongs, and they were often made *en suite* with flatware and cutlery services. Sugar sifters with pierced bowls were made for use with crushed sugar.

Francis Higgins & Sons was among the most prolific makers of cutlery in the 19th century. The firm was founded in 1782 by James Higgins and continued to produce silverware until 1940.

FLATWARE

DATE 1813

ASSAY TOWN London

MAKER William Chawner

LENGTH (tablespoon) 22cm (8¾in)

Cutlery, in both table and dessert sizes, began to be made in complete sets in the early 1800s. The fiddle pattern, which, with the stem spreading at the end, is thought to resemble a violin, had appeared in France by the late 17th century, and by the mid-18th century it was being made in many of the variations — with shell decorations and moulded or threaded edges — that were to become so well known throughout France and most other European countries. The shape was not introduced to England until c.1800, however, and the forks and spoons shown here are early examples. The fiddle pattern continued to dominate flatware in the 19th century, and in its plain form was made all over Europe and America. It sometimes bore die-stamped relief ornamentation, ranging from restrained designs to florid rococo.

William Chawner (d.1834) was a London spoonmaker, apprenticed in 1797 and freed in 1804, who registered seven marks between 1808 and 1833; these were either *WC* or *W·C* within a rectangle. After his death his widow, Mary, continued his business, and in 1840 she entered into partnership with her son-in-law George William Adams (1808–95).

FLATWARE

DATE c.1720

ASSAY TOWN London

MAKER Not known

LENGTH (knife) 27cm (10¾in)

The plain, rounded and up-turned terminal of these spoons and forks is known as the Hanoverian pattern, which first became popular c.1710 and fell from favour in the 1780s.

Flatware dating from mid-18th century onwards is comparatively readily available, although earlier examples are much rarer. The Restoration of the monarchy in 1660 saw the introduction of French styles to Britain, and forks came into widespread use, their old-fashioned cast finials being replaced by flattened handles, although they continued to have three prongs until the 1770s. These flat handles were ideal for displaying chased or stamped ornamentation, and they also made it possible to produce flatware quite cheaply because each piece could be made from one sheet of

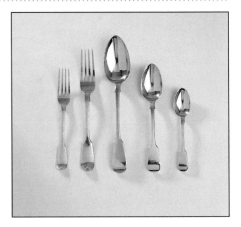

silver. Sets of matching pieces could also be easily manufactured, although it is now difficult to find sets together. One problem in trying to assemble a set of matching knives, forks and spoons is that many pieces will be engraved with the initials or crest of the original owners, so it is possible to tell at a glance if the set is genuine.

FLATWARE

DATE *c.* 1885

ASSAY TOWN New York

MAKER Tiffany & Co.

LENGTH (tablespoon) 22cm (8¾in)

Full services of flatware were first seen in America in the 1780s. In the early 19th century English flatware makers copied the French curving hour-glass pattern, but this did not prove popular. The design did, however, form the basis of the King's pattern (shown here), which appeared *c.*1815. The King's pattern is elaborate. The fiddle-shaped handle has scrolled and threaded edges with a scallop shell at the end and a pair of anthemion motifs along the stem.

Tiffany & Co., silver manufacturer and retailer, was founded in New York by Charles Louis Tiffany (1812–1902). Between 1837 and 1848 Tiffany was in partnership with John B. Young, trading as Tiffany & Young. In 1841 the firm became Tiffany, Young & Ellis, when J. L. Ellis was made a partner, and a decade later Tiffany made an arrangement with the company John C. Moore for the sole rights to distribute its silverware. Tiffany obtained sole control in 1853, when it became known as Tiffany & Co., and took over Edward C. Moore & Co. in 1868, a move that made Tiffany the most important silverware company in the United States.

Tiffany & Co. produced outstanding silver in Japanese, Indian and Moorish styles and, from the 1880s, ware in the art nouveau style. As well as a range of flatware, it made many presentation pieces. From 1902, under Louis Comfort Tiffany (1848–1933), the company was the leading exponent of art nouveau in the United States, and it created, in addition to its conventional lines, specialized "art jewellery".

CRUET

DATE 1767

ASSAY TOWN London

MAKER Charles Aldridge and Henry Greenaway

HEIGHT 18cm (7in)

DIAMETER 15cm (6in)

Frames to hold oil and vinegar bottles began to be made c.1720, and the earliest usually contained three casters and two bottles. However, some were made to hold two bottles – for oil and vinegar – although late 18th-century examples may contain as many as eight or even ten containers. This example has shell feet, and the motif is repeated on the back, central handle, a style that was replaced c.1770.

Charles Aldridge and Henry Green [*sic*] registered a joint mark, *C·A* sandwiched between *H* and *G* within a rounded cross-shape in 1775.

CRUET

DATE 1783

ASSAY TOWN London

MAKER William Sumner

HEIGHT 25cm (10in)

LENGTH 23cm (9in)

Glass-mounted bottles for all the condiments had become common by the 1770s and 1780s, and by the time this George III, eight-bottle engraved cruet set was made the preferred style of handle had become a centrally placed one, protruding above the bottles. The cut glass bottles sit in a base prettily engraved with swags of flowers and foliage interspersed with medallions. Footed, oval stands decorated in this style with pierced and bright cut ornamentation remained popular for about a decade.

CRUET

DATE *c.*1880
___

ASSAY TOWN Not known (probably Germany)
___

MAKER Berthold Müller
___

HEIGHT 12.5cm (5in)
___

This pair of salt and pepper holders is reminiscent of the porcelain figurines produced in Germany during the 19th century, where the close links of silversmiths with the porcelain industry enabled modellers to adapt their skills to both art forms.

Each piece is overmarked for Chester in 1910. The Customs Acts of 1842 made it illegal to import gold or silver articles into Britain and Ireland unless they had been assayed at a British assay office. From 1867, in addition to the usual British hallmarks, imported items were stamped with the letter *F* in an oval escutcheon, to indicate their foreign origin. Only items made before 1800 were exempt; after 1939 the exemption was extended to all items older than 100 years. From 1883 imported silver items had to be assayed at the office nearest to the point

of entry, which was usually either Chester or London. From 1904 imported pieces were marked with the decimal value of the fineness or standard of the silver within a horizontal oval – sterling silver with .925 and Britannia silver with .9584 – together with the date-letter and mark of the assay office.

Berthold Hermann Müller was an importer of German silver into Britain. In 1897 he used the initials *BM*, sometimes separate and sometimes conjoined, within a rectangular punch; in 1912 his mark was *B·H·M·* in a rectangle.

CRUET

DATE *c.*1870
___

ASSAY TOWN Paris
___

MAKER Not known
___

HEIGHT 28cm (11in)
___

WIDTH 30cm (12in)
___

The handles of the oil and vinegar bottles in this French cruet are of glass, unlike many British bottles, which had silver mounts and handles. The cruet itself is ornately decorated with foliage and bunches of grapes, and the central handle is in the form of a vine stem. The silver is 950 parts per 1,000.

SALT

DATE 1806

ASSAY TOWN London

MAKER Elizabeth Morley

HEIGHT 5cm (2in)

LENGTH 12.5cm (5in)

The beginning of the 19th century saw a growth of salts, sauce boats, tureens and entrée dishes made *en suite*.

This beautifully elegant salt is one of a pair. The low, boat-shaped bowl is decorated only with bands of reeding around the rim, and the decoration is repeated around the pedestal foot. Because salt, especially when damp, has a corrosive effect on silver, leading to the formation of silver chloride, the interiors of salts were generally gilded or, later, given blue glass liners.

This was also a popular shape for soup tureens, although they, of course, usually had covers.

MUSTARD POT

DATE 1857

ASSAY TOWN Sheffield

MAKER Henry Wilkinson & Co.

HEIGHT 7.5cm (3in)

DIAMETER 10cm (4in)

Until the late 18th century mustard was served in its dry form and was regarded as a spice, being offered from blind casters. Most of the silver pots used for mixed mustard have glass liners, which were easier to clean, and the silver is often pierced or decorated with open-work. If they were unlined, the interior would be gilded, as here. The gadrooning on the lid and around the body of the pot harks back to the decoration popular in the late 18th century.

This firm of manufacturing silversmiths was founded in Sheffield *c.*1830 by Henry Wilkinson, a plate worker, and it traded as Henry Wilkinson & Co. Its first mark was entered at Goldsmiths' Hall in 1857, and at that time the

company had a warehouse and showroom in London. From 1872 the firm traded as Henry Wilkinson & Co. Ltd, but it went into liquidation in 1892, when it was acquired by Walker & Hall.

SUGAR CASTER

DATE 1729

ASSAY TOWN London

MAKER Not known

HEIGHT 16.5cm (6½in)

Even at the height of the passion for the rococo the plain vase-type sugar caster remained popular – practicality for once outweighing fashion.

This George II vase-shaped sugar caster is typical of the casters made in the late 1720s and in the 1730s, with the decoration confined to the delicately pierced, alternately patterned panels of the cover. The marks on the top and base of a caster should coincide, and they are generally found on the bezel of the top (that is, the portion of the cover that fits inside the base) and under the foot.

DISH CROSS

DATE 1770

ASSAY TOWN London

MAKER Sarah Buttall

DIAMETER 30cm (12in)

These cross-shaped devices, which are sometimes called table crosses, were designed to support and keep a dish warm while protecting the table-top from the hot plate. They had a central spirit lamp, and the legs and arms, which rotate above each other, could be adjusted to hold dishes of different sizes.

They were made from the late 1730s until the end of the 18th century, being used to stand on the dinner-table or sideboard. They replaced the dish ring and were, in their turn, replaced by hot-water stands in the 19th century. American examples of dish crosses are extremely rare.

EGG CRUET

DATE 1812

ASSAY TOWN London

MAKER Paul Storr

HEIGHT 22cm (8½in)

WIDTH 24cm (9½in)

DEPTH 18.5cm (7¼in)

This fine cruet for six egg cups is rare. The egg cups have a band of anthemion (a stylized flower decoration) around the top, and, as is customary, the interiors are gilded to protect the silver from tarnishing and, of course, stains from egg yolks. The egg cups are held in a wire-work framework on a stand with a gadroon border and scroll feet.

The frame of egg cruets, which usually supported from four to six egg cups, sometimes also incorporated a container for salt and the appropriate number of egg spoons to complete the set.

Egg cups and, especially, egg spoons were usually gilded. In the 18th century this had been achieved by the process of fire gilding (known in France as *dorure d'or moulu*) – an amalgam (gold dissolved in mercury) was spread over the object, which was heated in a fire so that the mercury evaporated, leaving the gold fused to the surface of the silver. When it was found that mercury fumes were highly poisonous, electrolysis began to be used, and Rundell, Bridge & Rundell, for whom Storr had worked, was among the firms to pioneer the technique.

EGG CODDLER

DATE *c.* 1880

ASSAY TOWN Sheffield

MAKER Mappin Brothers

HEIGHT 22cm (8½in)

Egg coddlers or boilers were popular in Victorian times, when many were made in silver plate. They usually took the form of cylindrical or vase-shaped containers, with a flat or domed lid, which was sometimes divided into two hinged sections. The interiors were fitted with removable wire frames that could accommodate between four and eight eggs. Boiling water would be poured in and the burner below lighted. The coddler would be brought to the breakfast table, and, seven minutes later, the eggs would be ready to eat. The coddler illustrated, which holds four eggs, is plated.

Mappin Brothers was founded by the great-grandsons of Jonathan Mappin – Frederick Thorpe Mappin (1821– 1910), Edward Mappin (*d.* 1875), Joseph Charles Mappin (*d.* 1901) and John Newton Mappin (*d.* 1913).

Disagreements with his brothers caused John Newton Mappin to leave the family firm and found a company that eventually became Mappin & Webb. His brothers, trading as Mappin Brothers, acquired a cutlery firm in Sheffield, and their mark was entered at the Sheffield assay office in 1859. (See also page 42.)

TOAST RACK

DATE 1894

ASSAY TOWN London

MAKER Hodd & Sons

HEIGHT 18cm (7in)

DIAMETER 28cm (11in)

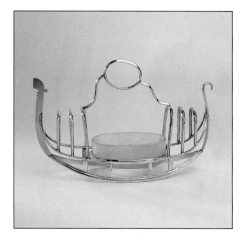

Toast racks do not seem to have been made before the late 18th century, and the earliest examples seem to have been little more than a single row of vertical pegs on a wire ring base. Later, circular wire loops (sometimes detachable) were used to separate the slices of toast. The stand, which could be oval or oblong, usually rested on four small feet and had a central vertical rod, surmounted by a ring handle.

This unusual toast rack, in the form of a gondola, shows the influence of the Arts & Crafts movement. Because of its intrinsic value, silver was not an immediately obvious material for proponents of the Arts & Crafts movement to use. However, in the late 19th century, increased production in Australia and the United States led to a fall in the price of silver – in 1888 it cost only 3 shillings and 7 pence an ounce. In 1890 gold, on the other hand, cost £4.4s.11½d an ounce, and the relative cheapness of silver made it a more attractive material for Arts & Crafts silversmiths.

DISH RING

DATE 1902

ASSAY TOWN Dublin

MAKER Not known

HEIGHT 23cm (9in)

DIAMETER 19cm (7½in) (top); 21cm (8¼in) (base)

These low, circular rings or bowls, with flat bases usually have concave sides. They were used in Ireland in much the same way as dish crosses were used in England – to support hot dishes and so protect table-tops from being marked. They were made for a time in the mid-18th century, but do not appear to have been made between 1790 and 1890. This reproduction is decorated with a rather crudely executed pierced and chased rustic scene.

The name "potato ring", which is sometimes given to dish rings, is a misnomer.

BOXES AND CADDIES

CASKET

DATE 1677

ASSAY TOWN London

MAKER Not known

LENGTH 22cm (8½in)

The lid of this oval Charles II casket is engraved with armorials within crossed plumes, and it is chased with roundels alternating with flutes and foliage. The rim is undulating, and the clasp is pierced. The compressed sides are chased in the same style as the lid, and the casket rests on four scroll supports. It is marked with *C* over *W*, but the maker is not known.

Oval, bun-shaped caskets with a hinged lid secured by a hasp and mounted on four scrolled feet and dating from the mid-17th century are often called sugar boxes, although they may also have been used for jewellery or sweetmeats. Like spice boxes, they were superseded by the caster.

TOILET BOXES

DATE 1678–9

ASSAY TOWN Mons

MAKER Hubert Horion-Dore

DIMENSIONS 20 x 12.5 x 7.5cm (8 x 5 x 3in)

By the 1680s the gauge used for silver throughout northern Europe had increased, and applied and cast ornament was widely used. This pair of silver embossed and chased toilet boxes from Belgium shows the finest quality decoration in the naturalistic baroque style of northern Europe before the domination of baroque.

Pattern-books such as *Livre nouveau de fleurs très util pour l'art d'orfèvrerie et autres* (1645) by the Parisian engraver Nicolas Cochin (1610–86), which depicts naturalistic flowers for engraving on silver and small and delicate landscapes and battles, helped to establish an effuse, floral-foliate style of embossing and chasing, often open-worked. French workmanship became ascendant and enjoyed a primacy in Europe for two centuries, influencing the styles used in neighbouring countries.

Tea Caddies and Sugar Box

DATE 1738

ASSAY TOWN London

MAKER Paul de Lamerie

HEIGHT 15cm (6in)

From the late 1730s it became usual for tea caddies to be made in sets. This set of two tea caddies and a slightly larger sugar box is by one of London's premier silversmiths and a leading exponent of the rococo style. The cast and chased decorations have been executed to the highest standards. These caddies were designed to be kept in a lockable, probably shagreen-covered case because tea was a rare and expensive commodity at the time, and the finials are hinged so that the depth of the case could be reduced.

One of the most famous silversmiths ever to have worked in Britain, Paul de Lamerie (1688–1751) produced highly collectable and expensive pieces. Born in the Netherlands to French parents, he was one of the many Huguenot refugees to settle in London, where he was apprenticed to his fellow-countryman Pierre Platel (c.1664–1719) in 1703, registering his mark, *LA*, a star and a larger crown above and a fleur-de-lys below, in 1713. In 1732 he registered the mark *P·L* below a crown and a star and above a stylized fleur-de-lys. In 1739 the mark was a cursive *PL* below a crown and above a small circle.

His early work was formal and mostly in the plain, rather flat-surfaced Queen Anne style, which was ideal for engraving, alternating with broad flutes and sharp angles. During the 1730s, however, he adopted a flamboyant rococo style, and by 1740 he had become one of the style's prime exponents, producing lavishly decorated masterpieces of exuberantly executed casting and chasing.

De Lamerie settled in Soho, London, where he made both splendid, immensely valuable pieces, some for royal clients, as well as humbler, more domestic objects. All were well made, however, and of heavy gauge silver, and some of the more spectacular items were finely engraved with armorials, work that may have been carried out by William Hogarth (1697–1764). Much of his work survives, which suggests that his workshops were among the most prolific in London.

TEA CADDY

DATE 1714

ASSAY TOWN London

MAKER possibly Thomas Parr

HEIGHT 12cm (4¾in)

This octagonal tea caddy has sliding shoulders and a detachable bun cover. Simple, straight-sided octagons – rectangles with the corners cut off – were among the most popular shapes for early caddies, and they were similar in form to the original porcelain Chinese tea jars, although oval, rectangular and inverted baluster shapes were also made.

Individual caddies were made, but they were often made in sets of two or sometimes three, the third being for sugar, and they were designed to fit into a lockable box, for tea was an expensive luxury – both scarce and heavily taxed. They were usually flat topped with a central hole with a domed cover, which was used as a measure.

TEA CADDY

DATE 1785

ASSAY TOWN London

MAKER Thomas Crippin

HEIGHT 15cm (6in)

WIDTH 15cm (6in)

This single, lockable, fluted caddy is simply decorated with bright cut engraving but is topped by a rather unattractive, stained ivory, pineapple-shaped finial.

By the late 18th century tea caddies were often made with two internal divisions for black and green tea, a style that obviated the need for an outer, lockable case because the caddy itself could be fitted with a key.

Caddies should bear a full set of marks on the body, while the lid should be marked with the lion passant and the maker's mark.

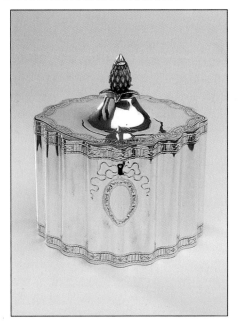

TEA CADDY

DATE 1795

ASSAY TOWN London

MAKER John Scofield

HEIGHT 14cm (5½in)

WIDTH 13cm (5¼in)

John Scofield (or Schofield, *fl.*1776–96) entered his first mark in 1776, when he was in partnership with Robert Jones. In 1778 he entered a second mark, this time alone, and in 1787 a third. He has been said to have been one of the finest designers and craftsmen of the period, specializing in candlesticks and candelabra and excelling in mounting glass. His considerable output also included tureens, tea urns, coffee pots and hot water jugs, and much of his work was in the Adam style, sometimes decorated with medallions. He was especially interested in the ways in which light was reflected from the surfaces of the pieces he made. He may have worked for Jeffreys, Jones & Gilbert, Goldsmiths to the Crown at the time, and may also have made silverware for Carlton House (the home of George IV while he was Prince of Wales).

This oval, lockable tea caddy has bands of bright cut engraving at the top and base, and the design is repeated around the edge of the lid, which is topped by an ivory finial (also known as a *knop*).

TEA CADDY

DATE 1864

ASSAY TOWN London

MAKER Frederick Brasted

HEIGHT 14cm (5½in) (including finial)

WIDTH 13.5cm (5¼in)

DEPTH 9.5cm (3¾in)

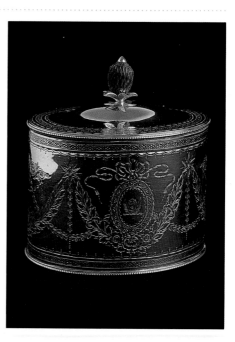

Although this caddy was made in the style of the 1790s, by the mid-19th century tea had become a much less valuable commodity, and there was no longer any need for lockable lids.

Frederick Brasted (or Brastead, *d.*1888) was in partnership with John Bell from 1857 until 1862, the firm being known as Bell & Brasted. After 1862 Brasted worked on his own, his mark being a simple *FB* within a rectangle with canted corners. After his death the business was continued by his widow, Susannah, and, from 1895, by his son, Harry.

BISCUIT BARREL

DATE *c.*1865

ASSAY TOWN Sheffield

MAKER Akin Brothers

HEIGHT 20cm (8in)

This biscuit barrel with a hinged lid and hand-chased, somewhat florid decorations set against a mottled ground and interspersed with circular medallions is typical of the kind made in Britain at this period. A few examples were made in sterling silver, but most were, like the one shown here, made of silver plate. They are popular with collectors in both the US and Britain, and many have found their way to the USA.

A full set of marks should appear on the body, while the cover should bear a lion passant and the maker's mark.

BISCUIT BOX

DATE *c.*1870

ASSAY TOWN Sheffield

MAKER Fenton Brothers

HEIGHT 23cm (9in)

DIAMETER 15cm (6in)

This hinged and folding biscuit box has the stylized bark framework that was so popular at this period. The interior grilles slot neatly into the centre when the biscuit box is fully open. These pieces were often used for nuts, berries or sweetmeats.

The brothers John Frederick and Frank Fenton first registered their mark with the Sheffield assay office in 1875, at the same time registering a mark with the London assay office, and giving as their address their London showrooms in Bartletts Buildings near Holborn Circus. By 1883 John Frederick had either retired or died and Frank had retired, and John Frederick's son, Samuel Fenton, had taken over the firm.

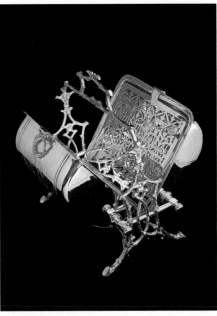

Vinaigrette

DATE 1836

ASSAY TOWN Birmingham

MAKER Nathaniel Mills

DIMENSIONS 3 x 4.5cm (1¼ x 1¾in)

Vinaigrettes are small boxes, made to hold a sponge soaked in a perfumed liquid and concealed under a grille. They first appeared c.1810 ·

The interior grilles were generally decorated with a pierced and engraved pattern of flowers and scrolls. Many early 19th-century vinaigrettes were hardly more than 2.5cm (1in) long, and these tiny examples had simple dot-pierced grilles and engraved tops.

In the 1830s vinaigrettes became larger and more ornate. Many were made to commemorate events such as Admiral Nelson's victory in 1805 at Trafalgar or the Great Exhibition of 1851. Others celebrated popular authors such as Lord Byron (1788–1824) and Sir Walter Scott (1771–1832) by being made in the form of a book with the author's name on the spine.

Many vinaigrettes were decorated with a plaque, inserted in the flat, rectangular hinged lid, depicting a scene of a British castle such as Windsor or Kenilworth, Byron's home at Newstead Abbey, or, as in the rare box shown here, a manor house such as Abbotsford House, the home of Sir Walter Scott. Some were decorated with scenes of cathedrals or monuments. Such pieces are known as castle-top ware, and the best examples are cast in high relief; second-rate ones are die-stamped and then finished with hand chasing.

The market for these small pieces was dominated by Birmingham smallware manufacturers, known as toymakers. Although Birmingham had long had a reputation for producing shoddy, mass-produced wares of poor quality, the best of the snuff boxes were generally beautifully constructed, with well-concealed joints and firm hinges.

SNUFF BOX

DATE c.1770

ASSAY TOWN Paris

MAKER Not known

DIMENSIONS 4 x 10cm (1½ x 4in)

In 16th-century France, taking snuff was considered beneficial to the health, and the custom spread to England in the 17th century. It is often difficult to distinguish between early 18th-century tobacco and snuff boxes, although conventionally tobacco boxes are larger, while some snuff boxes have two internal compartments.

Shapes varied widely, as did the extent and quality of the engraved decoration, which could be simple, rather formal or lavishly pictorial – complex scenes of cavalry combat are not unknown – although these were generally embossed on separate plates that were soldered to the lids. In the late 18th and early 19th centuries they were generally rectangular and often decorated with simple, engine-turned ornamentation.

SNUFF BOX

DATE 1832

ASSAY TOWN Birmingham

MAKER Nathaniel Mills

DIMENSIONS 8 x 5 x 2.5cm (3¼ x 2 x 1in)

Snuff boxes were often used for presentations, and this one bears the inscription: "Presented to Mr Gavin Scott by the Corporation of Sons of Freemen Bakers in testimony of their gratitude for his unwearied exertion to promote the interests of the Corporation. Glasgow 27th June 1833".

In the 19th century small silver articles and trinkets for everyday use – caddy spoons, buckles, boxes and buttons, nutmeg graters, wine labels, card cases, vinaigrettes and so on – were known as "toys", and Birmingham was known as "the toy-making capital of the world". Among the leading makers were Joseph Willmore, Samuel Pendleton, Joseph Taylor and, especially, Nathaniel Mills (fl. 1826–50).

SNUFF BOX

DATE 1845

ASSAY TOWN Moscow

MAKER Not known

DIMENSIONS 2.5 x 9cm (1 x 3½in)

Niello was widely used in continental Europe, especially Russia c.1770–1870, to enhance scroll-work designs. It is a black or grey compound, usually made of one part copper to one part silver and two parts lead or of equal parts of sulphur, lead and mercury, which was used to fill the engraved detail. The line incised into the metal is triangular in section, the apex usually opening on the surface of the metal as a narrow line so that the alloy could be "locked" into position. The compound was spread over and into the design and heated, the excess being polished away. In England in the early 19th century it was sometimes used to black in names on bottle tickets. The technique is an ancient one, Benvenuto Cellini (1500–71) having claimed to have revived it from a forgotten art.

CIGAR CASE

DATE 1909

ASSAY TOWN Birmingham

MAKER Not known

DIMENSIONS 13 x 10cm (5¼ x 4in)

Cigars were introduced into Europe by the Spanish soon after the discovery of America and the first factory to make cigars was opened in Hamburg in 1788. The taste for cigar smoking had become well-established in Britain by the end of the century, and throughout the 19th and early 20th centuries the Birmingham "toymakers" or smallware makers produced dozens of different designs in a variety of sizes, ranging from large, table-top boxes to slim cases to be carried in the pocket.

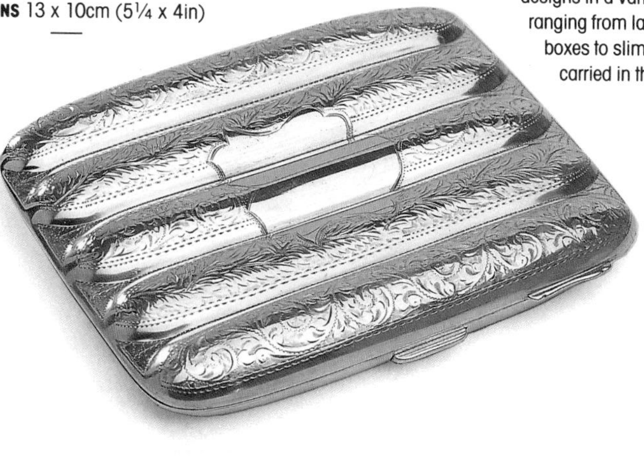

CASKET

DATE 1905

ASSAY TOWN Birmingham

MAKER Charles S. Green & Co.

HEIGHT 10cm (4in)

LENGTH 25cm (10in)

Boxes are normally marked on a top in addition to a full set of marks being applied to the base. Marks that appear on the side should be treated with caution.

The bombe shape – a swelling or convex surface – was widely used for cabinet furniture made in the baroque style, especially Dutch and French furniture made in the early 18th century. The shape was also popular for rococo-style teapots, tea caddies, tureens and caskets. This ornate little bombe casket, which stands on four small, plain feet, has a frieze of figures running around the sides and across the lid.

JEWELLERY BOX

DATE 1905

ASSAY TOWN Birmingham

MAKER Liberty & Co.

DIMENSIONS 5 x 10 x 10cm (2 x 4 x 4in)

In 1875 Arthur Lasenby Liberty (1843–1917) opened his famous emporium for oriental silks, Japanese porcelain, fans, screens and so on in Regent Street, London, and he was quick to adopt all new fashions, buying in Japanese products and commissioning Japanese-style articles. When enthusiasm for japonaiserie waned Liberty turned to the Arts & Crafts movement but soon found the modifications to that rather austere style that followed from art nouveau more to his liking.

In 1898–9 Liberty established his company's new Cymric range for silver and jewellery, which was produced by William Hair Haseler & Co., a Birmingham manufacturer of jewellery and silverware. From 1901 such artists as Bernard Cuzner (1877–1956), Arthur Gaskin (1862–1928), Archibald Knox (1864–1933)

and Rex Silver (1879–1965) were designing objects for the Cymric range, although the names of individual designers were not identified. Another notable Liberty designer was Scottish-born Jessie Marion King (1875–1949).

This box, with its enamel and turquoise matrix, is typical of the range. Birmingham-made Liberty pieces bear the mark *L & Co* within three conjoined diamonds (this mark was registered in 1903). London-made ware bear the mark *Ly & Co.* within a rectangle with canted corners (this mark was registered in 1899).

SHELL-SHAPED BOX

DATE 1913

ASSAY TOWN London

MAKER Sebastian Garrard

HEIGHT 6.5cm (2½in)

LENGTH 15cm (6in)

This shell-shaped box is very similar to the small silver caskets in the shape of scallop shells, which were made in the late 16th and early 17th centuries and which are usually called "spice boxes". In most examples there are internal partitions, forming separate compartments. They were mounted on small shell or snail feet, and the convex lids bore radiating, embossed ribs in the style of the shells, while the low, vertical sides follow the shape of the lid. Boxes shaped like scallop shells but without the internal compartments are often called sugar boxes.

Sebastian Henry Garrard (1868–1946), the son of James Mortimer Garrard, entered his first mark in 1889 and worked in the family business R. & S. Garrard & Co.

SWISS SINGING BIRD BOX

DATE 1920s

ASSAY TOWN Not known (Switzerland)

MAKER Not known

DIMENSIONS 4 x 10 x 5.5cm (1½ x 4 x 2¼in)

This silver gilt, enamelled singing bird box has a watch let into the front. Apparently only 1,000 were made – this one is marked 676. The bird sings and rotates and then disappears back into its box.

Geneva was the centre of the Swiss watch and automata trade, and enamelled snuff boxes and music boxes from that city often incorporate watches and automata. Many of the brightly enamelled gold boxes made in Switzerland were intended for the east European market. Although this example is simply decorated, boxes were enamelled with exotic flowers or allegorical and pastoral scenes, often within complex geometric borders.

CANDLESTICKS AND CANDELABRA

SCONCES

DATE 1622

ASSAY TOWN Utrecht

MAKER Adam van Vianen

HEIGHT 35.5cm (14in)

WIDTH 24cm (9½in)

Although the name is sometimes applied to ordinary candlesticks or candelabra, a sconce is usually a wall-mounted candle holder, often in the form of a cartouche, with two or more projecting branches. The embossed and open-work design of these wall sconces exploits both the reflective properties of silver and the sculptural skills of the silversmith. They were made at the height of the auricular period, anticipating the Dutch baroque.

Adam van Vianen (c. 1565–1627), who was born in Utrecht and worked there throughout his life, was the son of a goldsmith and himself became a master goldsmith in 1593. He worked with his brother Paul (c. 1570–1613) and evolved a fleshy Mannerist style.

CHAMBERSTICK

DATE 1770

ASSAY TOWN London

MAKER Ebenezer Coker

HEIGHT 10cm (4in)

DIAMETER 19cm (7½in)

Candlesticks on dished stands with a ring handle or a longer, spoon-like handle fixed to the rim were originally called low-footed candlesticks, but sometimes also flat candlesticks, chambersticks, bedroom candlesticks or hand candlesticks.

The basic style changed little over the years. Most have circular, shallow, saucer-like trays, although octagonal and rectangular ones were made, and they were simply decorated, if at all. This example has a beaded border. From the mid-18th century almost all chambersticks were made with an accompanying conical extinguisher, which usually ended in a small knob finial.

Ebenezer Coker (1738–c. 70) worked in London, registering various cursive *EC* marks. He favoured the classical style, and his plain, neat work is often decorated with bright cut engraving. In addition to candlesticks, he made salvers and waiters, some with cast and pierced applied borders.

CHAMBERSTICKS

DATE 1794

ASSAY TOWN London

MAKER Elizabeth Jones

HEIGHT 11.5cm (4½in)

DIAMETER 18cm (7in)

These plain George III chambersticks with their original snuffers are simply decorated with bands of

reeding around the slightly up-turned edge of the pan and on the shaft. The snuffers or extinguishers were usually made with a short vertical prong on one side which fitted into a socket attached to the shaft or, as here, the handle.

Chambersticks were often made in pairs or in sets of four or more, and it is likely that most householders would have possessed as many, if not more, chambersticks as candlesticks. Now, however, they are less often seen.

CHAMBERSTICKS

DATE 1856/7

ASSAY TOWN London

MAKER R. & S. Garrard & Co.

DIAMETER 14cm (5½in)

The bases of chambersticks, which serve as drip pans, were usually undecorated, but some, such as those shown here, have moulded, up-curved rims; others are decorated with reeding, beading or gadrooning. A few rest on small feet. The lug handles of this set of 12 are engraved with a crest and coronet.

Until 1720 chambersticks were marked on the top of the tray, in a straight or curved line, but after that date they were marked underneath.

CANDLESTICKS

DATE 1702

ASSAY TOWN London

MAKER Edward Ironside

HEIGHT (candlesticks) 16cm (6¼in)

HEIGHT (snuffers stand) 12cm (4¾in)

These silver gilt Queen Anne candlesticks and snuffers stand have partially matted, circular bases and knopped stems, embossed or cast with bold gadroons. The simplicity of line, with the sunken, bell-shaped bases and baluster columns, is typical of this period. All three pieces are engraved with the same coat of arms within husk-festooned, scroll cartouches.

Also shown are a pair of silver-gilt snuffers, made in London in 1715 by David Green, which are engraved with identical armorials to those on the candlesticks and stand. Snuffers, scissor-like implements used for trimming and extinguishing candles, have a cutting edge for trimming the candles, and a box-like section at the end of the blade collected the snuffed wick. Not all scissor-type candle snuffers incorporate a wick trimmer. David Green's 1701 mark was *Gr* below a crown; in 1720 it was *DG* in a rectangle.

CANDLESTICKS

DATE 1751

ASSAY TOWN London

MAKER William Homer

HEIGHT 20.5cm (8¼in)

WIDTH 14cm (5½in) (at base)

This pair of cast candlesticks is decorated with six shells around the base, and the hexagonal motif is repeated on the wax pan.

By the reign of George II (1727–60) candlesticks had become taller and rather spindly. In the early 18th century they were usually no taller than 18cm (7in); by the middle years of the century they could be up to 25cm (10in) tall; and by 1775 they could be 30cm/12in tall. After this time they became rather shorter, averaging 23–28cm (9–11in). The base, stem and sconce of candlesticks were usually cast in separate moulds and soldered together, and cast examples are more keenly sought after than "loaded" candlesticks – ones made from thin sheets of silver and filled with pitch (tar) or plaster of Paris to make them heavy.

Cast candlesticks are usually marked underneath, with one stamp on each corner or at the side of square bases or with the marks in a line near the centre of circular bases. Sometimes one of a pair of candlesticks will have been cast from the other.

CANDLESTICKS

DATE *c.*1797
—
ASSAY TOWN Paris
—
MAKER Not known
—
HEIGHT 30cm (12in)

These first quality, rare, cast candlesticks were made in silver of 950 parts per 1,000. The formality of the design is typical of the style associated with the furnishings popular during the reign of Louis XIV and with the austere, rather severe style seen in the early paintings of Jacques-Louis David (1748–1825).

French candlesticks were normally cast in three sections – two vertical sections and the base – and the casting technique was also used for some larger items of furniture.

CANDELABRUM

DATE 1884
—
ASSAY TOWN Birmingham
—
MAKER Elkington & Co.
—
HEIGHT 53cm (21in)
—
SPREAD 38cm (15in)
—

This is one of a pair of four-light candelabra, ornately decorated with cast flowers and foliage. Elkington & Co., which operated from the 1840s to the mid-1900s, was based in Birmingham, but its wares may bear the mark of other towns. It made its reputation initially by electroplating, for which it held the patent. It also made a massive quantity of sterling silver articles of every type. The company's success enabled it to hire the best designers for its superbly made articles, which ranged from the day-to-day to the important. During the late 19th century there was great interest in Japanese art and decoration, and engraved birds, flowers and butterflies, handles resembling bamboo and fan-shaped trays enjoyed wide popularity. Elkington made use not only of Japanese designs but also Japanese techniques – for example, it used cloisonné enamelling on silver or, more often, its electrotype wares. The company's pre-eminence was largely the result of its virtual monopoly of electroplate. It also produced electrotypes – copies of objects (usually copper) made by electrodeposition, which were then electroplated in silver. (See also page 74.)

MISCELLANEOUS PIECES

PORRINGER

DATE 1683

ASSAY TOWN London

MAKER Not known

DIAMETER 11cm (4¼in)

These shallow vessels were originally made to contain pottage (or porridge), semi-liquid food. Many porringers, both in silver and pewter, have survived from the second half of the 17th and the early 18th centuries.

In the 17th and 18th centuries, when bleeding was considered to be of therapeutic value in the treatment of a variety of ailments, shallow silver (sometimes pewter) bowls with single lugs or handles, similar to the piece shown here, were often used. Such bowls, which are sometimes called cupping bowls, were not specially made for the purpose; they were ordinary porringers, engraved on the inside with rings of graduated lines to measure the quantity of blood taken. Bowls without such engraved lines should not be called bleeding bowls, and true bleeding bowls have a capacity of no more than 85ml/3fl oz. This bowl, a type made in England only between 1625 and 1730, was marked *HT*.

WINE TASTER

DATE 1741

ASSAY TOWN Lyon

MAKER Not known

DIAMETER 9cm (3½in) (excluding handle)

The basic French form of wine taster, which was also sometimes made in England, usually has one flat, horizontal handle, level with the rim and supported by a second, vertical ring, which is held by the thumb and forefinger; a few examples, including this one, have a single, horizontal ring handle. There is characteristically a slightly bossed bottom and dimpled recesses or hollow gadrooning to "break the wine" so that when it was swirled, the colour and clarity of the wine can be gauged. Most are between 7.5cm (3in) and 10cm (4in) in diameter. They often have thick walls, and many are decorated with a spray of leaves around the side.

Wine tasters would have been owned by anyone who had professional contact with wine, including butlers and vintners. English examples are, however, comparatively rare; they were far more common in France, especially among wine producers.

BEAKER

DATE c. 1865

ASSAY TOWN Not known (Netherlands)

MAKER Not known

HEIGHT 23cm (9in)

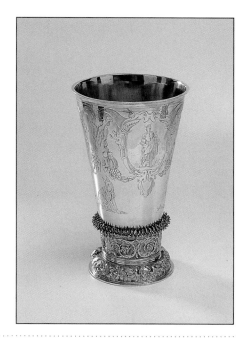

This is a re-creation of a piece dating from 1655–6 by Hindrick (or Hinrich) Muntinck of Groningen, who was probably the brother of the goldsmith and engraver Adrian Muntinck. The original may be seen in the Rijksmuseum, Amsterdam.

The beaker is probably the oldest form of man-made drinking vessel, and it, rather than the standing cup, was the characteristic north European drinking vessel in the 16th and 17th centuries. After the Reformation it tended to supplant the chalice in communion services. They were often decorated with religious motifs, and the foot was sometimes strengthened with bands of stamped and moulded silver.

PAP BOAT

DATE 1819

ASSAY TOWN London

MAKER William Bateman

LENGTH 13.5cm (5¼in)

WIDTH 7.5cm (3in)

These small receptacles for feeding pap (a soft food made of bread cooked in milk) to infants and invalids are usually boat-shaped, and the feeding end is shaped as a short or extended, tapering lip, which could be placed in the mouth of the person being fed. They do not usually have handles, although a few were made with flat handles or with vertical loop handles. Some are circular, and some have a fixed cover extending over either the holding end or the feeding portion. They were made between c. 1700 and c. 1830, and most were practical and plain. From c. 1800 a rim wire was sometimes applied, and from the mid-18th century a narrow band of bright cut engraving was occasionally used as a simple decoration. Some pap boats have been converted into cream jugs by the addition of three feet and a handle.

William Bateman (1774–1850), the grandson of Hester Bateman (see page 28), used either *WB* or *W·B* in a canted-corner or curved rectangular shape.

NUTMEG GRATER

DATE 1784

—

ASSAY TOWN London

—

MAKER Thomas Phipps and Edward Robinson

—

DIMENSIONS 2 x 5cm (¾ x 2in)

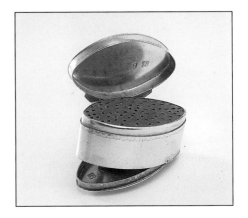

Nutmeg was widely used in the 17th and 18th centuries to improve the taste of ale, to enhance the flavours of a range of foods and drinks and, above all, as an ingredient of punch. Nutmeg graters, which are now rather rare items, were made throughout the 17th and 18th centuries and into the early 19th century. The earliest ones are in the form of a simple box with a hinged lid and base, an inset steel grater and a space within the box to contain the whole nut. In the late 17th century some cylindrical examples were made, with a cylindrical silver or steel grater, although silver is not sufficiently robust to grate nutmeg, and some vase-shaped graters, decorated with bright cut engraving were produced. Among the trifles made by smallworkers or toymakers during the second half of the 18th century and into the 19th century were egg-shaped, mace-like cases, frequently with a corkscrew concealed in a long, tubular base and with a space to hold the nutmeg, with the grater fixed and hinged below the cover.

Thomas Phipps and Edward Robinson (*fl. c.* 1784–1814) were well-known makers of miniature silver, especially nutmeg graters, snuff boxes, wine labels and so on. In 1783 they registered the mark *TP* and *ER*.

LEMON STRAINER

DATE 1756

—

ASSAY TOWN London

—

MAKER Not known

—

DIMENSIONS 11 x 9cm (4¼ x 3½in) (excluding handle)

Citrus fruits – orange, lemon and lime – were an essential ingredient of punch, and silver was the only known ware (apart from glazed pottery and porcelain) that could be used without taint. From *c.* 1680 strainers with long tubular handles began to appear; the holes were usually simply dot-pierced. By the early 18th century more intricate scroll and flower head piercing became popular, with two handles cut and pierced in similar scrolling patterns. Other strainers have solid handles; some have wirework handles. From the middle of the 18th century geometrically dot-pierced patterns were usual, and this functional example is so decorated.

STIRRUP CUPS

DATE 1805

ASSAY TOWN London

MAKER Not known

LENGTH 14cm (5½in)

Originally a stirrup cup was the drink offered on departure, but it has become associated with hunting, and nearly all the earliest recorded 18th-century stirrup cups take the form of fox heads, a few actually being made of fox skulls mounted in silver. Some were modelled on hares or stags.

The earliest examples are often flatter than a real-life fox, and they often show the fox with bared teeth. Although later versions tend to be more realistic, the forward-pointing ears of the foxes of this pair of cups give a faintly quizzical expression – most were, in fact, made with ears that lie back along the head to avoid awkward projections. The fox's fur was rendered with varying degrees of realism. Smaller versions were made from c. 1800 as snuff boxes.

CHAFING DISH

DATE c. 1870

ASSAY TOWN London

MAKER Martin, Hall & Co. Ltd

HEIGHT 19cm (7½in)

DIAMETER 26.5cm (10½in)

A chafing dish was a silver or, as here, silver-plated serving bowl with a handle and cover, often rectangular with rounded corners, designed to be placed over a spirit lamp or other heat source to keep food warm. The handles are usually detachable. Many chafing dishes have hot-water jackets (i.e., they are double-skinned) and were used to serve hors d'oeuvres or vegetables. The cover of the dish illustrated is hand-engraved.

The Sheffield-based firm of Martin, Hall & Co. Ltd was founded by John Roberts, who traded with Henry Wilkinson as Wilkinson & Roberts. In 1836, when Wilkinson resigned from the partnership, Roberts started working with Ebenezer Hall, with whom he formed a partnership in 1846, when the firm was known as Roberts & Hall. In 1854 Roberts & Hall joined forces with the firm of Martin & Naylor to form Martin, Hall & Co. The company ceased trading in 1936.

WINE COASTERS

DATE 1797

ASSAY TOWN London

MAKER John Terry

HEIGHT 4.5cm (1¾in)

DIAMETER 14.5cm (5¾in)

The name coaster derives from the practice of passing the bottle or decanter of port or brandy around the table after dinner, when it was the custom to remove the tablecloth before the dessert was served, and the wooden, baize-covered base of the coaster protected the table-top. The first coasters appeared c.1760, and they were often made by specialist makers of baskets and cruets. They were generally made in pairs or sets of four (sometimes more) and had pierced, vertical sides, 4–5cm (1½–2in) high, strengthened by gadroons or wire mounts, sometimes shaped and pierced in a variety of scrolling designs. By c.1770 the fashion for neoclassicism dictated that coasters should have vertical pales, festoons,

medallions, vases and geometrical motifs. Towards the end of the century, however, larger, often unpierced coasters became fashionable, but these were quickly followed by fluted and boldly gadrooned examples, similar to those shown here.

Coasters are usually marked on the base, although some early and late 18th-century examples and those made in the early 19th century were marked on the side.

WINE COOLERS

DATE 1840

ASSAY TOWN London

MAKER Benjamin Smith Jr

HEIGHT 26.5cm (10½in)

These fine quality sterling silver wine coolers were made for presentation to Sir Thomas Phillips to mark his stand against the Chartists, who had held a National Convention to press their demands for economic and political reform very near to the Houses of Parliament in 1839. The stylized, wavy rims illustrate the rococo revival, and the encrusted vine and shell-like decorations mark revivalist, rather than the true, rococo spirit.

Wine coolers, for holding iced water to chill one or more bottles of wine, were made, often in pairs or sets of four or more, to stand on a sideboard. At first, in the 1790s, they had straight sides, tapering slightly outwards to a flat base; some barrel-shaped coolers were made, decorated with encircling hoops. Later they were made with footed bases, decorated around the bottom with

gadrooning and with two upward-slanting horizontal handles or two drop-ring handles. Some, like those shown here, were shaped like an urn or inverted bell, with two side handles like a Greek krater (wide-mouthed urn) of the calyx type.

Benjamin Smith (1793–1850) was the eldest son of Benjamin Smith (1764–1823), with whom he entered his first mark in 1816. He supplied prototypes to Elkington & Co. for electroplating until 1849, and his later work featured flowers, leaves and other natural objects in a naturalistic, organic style. He was succeeded by his son, Stephen (fl.1850–86).

WINE CISTERN

DATE 1893

ASSAY TOWN London

MAKER Lambert & Co.

HEIGHT 25cm (10in)

LENGTH 63.5cm (25in)

WIDTH 30cm (12in)

Wine cisterns, or, more accurately, wine coolers, were made in silver from the time of the Restoration (1660), although examples in pewter were made before that time. Although they are all of basically the same shape, they vary enormously in size. Their original purpose was to hold cold water in which bottles or decanters of wine could be cooled, and small examples about 50cm/20in long and 30cm/12in high were presumably intended to hold two bottles. Some vessels, although known as wine cisterns, were large enough to be used as baths — one famous example made by Charles Kandler of London, which was bought by the Empress Catherine II of Russia, is 1.79m (5ft 9in) wide (including the handles), and the Sutherland cistern, made by Paul de Lamerie in 1738, is 96.5cm (38in) wide.

The firm of Lambert & Co. was founded c.1788 by Francis Lambert (c.1778–1841), who had sold jewellery and silver plate from a shop in Coventry Street, London. By the latter years of the 19th century the firm was run by Francis Lambert's second son, Geroge (d.1901).

BOTTLE TICKETS

DATE 1811

ASSAY TOWN London

MAKER Paul Storr

DIMENSIONS 7.5 x 5cm (3 x 2in)

These very heavy, very fine quality silver gilt wine labels are lavishly decorated with bunches of grapes and foliage. Labels suspended on thin chains around the necks of decanters and pierced or engraved with the name of the contents are often called wine labels. In fact, since the decanters frequently held whisky, brandy or port, or even strong ale, bottle ticket is a more appropriate and accurate name. They were first made in the 1730s, and the earliest examples were in the form of an escutcheon; these early tickets usually bore only the mark of the maker and the quality mark (usually sterling). Fully marked ones began to appear in the 1790s.

INKSTAND

DATE 1837

ASSAY TOWN London

MAKER Mary and Richard Sibley

HEIGHT 12.5cm (5in)

LENGTH 40cm (16in)

WIDTH 29cm (11½in)

Inkstands were rarely made before the last decades of the 17th century, but they were very popular throughout the 18th and 19th centuries, when they were made of silver, Sheffield plate and, sometimes, pewter. Glass bottles for ink began to appear in the mid-18th century. Inkstands can be very complicated pieces or very simple. They may include pots for ink and sand, a receptacle for wafers, a bell, a wax jack and a taperstick (small candlestick), all contained on a tray, which was usually rectangular and which may have had a trough to hold the pen or quill. They were popular and necessary pieces of equipment for libraries and writing tables, and they were often given as presentation pieces, when they were suitably engraved. All detachable parts should bear the maker's mark and a lion passant.

Richard Sibley (*fl.* 1829–80) was the son of an established London silversmith, also Richard, to whom he was apprenticed, and on his father's death in 1836 he became a business partner of his mother, Mary. By 1837, however, he appears to have been trading on his own account. In 1836 Richard Sibley and Mary Sibley registered the mark *M·R* above *S* within a heart.

INKSTAND

DATE *c.* 1851

ASSAY TOWN Birmingham

MAKER Elkington, Mason & Co.

DIAMETER 23.5cm (9¼in)

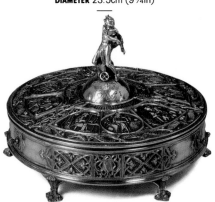

This circular, parcel-gilt, electroplated, copper electrotype inkstand is based on the design executed by John Leighton (1822–1912) for the Commemorative Shield of the Great Exhibition of 1851. The central glass inkwell has a detachable cover in the form of a terrestrial glove, with the figure of Mercury hovering above the North Pole. It is surrounded by relief vignettes of figures representing "raw materials", "manufactures" and "commerce" within a border of the names of artists within a gothic trellis. The sides are fitted with three wooden drawers (numbered 19, 20 and 21) above six gothic ruffle supports.

George Richards Elkington (1801–65) and his cousin and business partner Henry Elkington (*c.* 1810–52) took out patents – in 1836 and 1838 – on the subject of electrogilding, the process of coating a base metal with gold by electrolysis, and during the next few years G.R. Elkington bought up the patents of all the technical improvements devised by his contemporaries, including in 1840 a patent for a system of electroplating devised by John Wright of Birmingham. In the 1840s G.R. and H. Elkington formed a partnership with Josiah Mason (*d.* 1859). By 1845 the company had introduced a method of producing electrotypes, exact copies of objects (usually in copper) made by electrodeposition, which were then electroplated in silver.

INKSTAND

DATE 1901
___

ASSAY TOWN London
___

MAKER William Hutton & Co. Ltd
___

DIMENSIONS 23 x 10 x 10cm (9 x 4 x 4in)
___

The art nouveau pattern is hand-chased onto the silver base and each of the compressed ball green inkwells is surmounted by a hinged circular silver cover with flattened, open-work mounts.

This firm of silversmith and electroplaters was established in Sheffield in 1832 by William Carr Hutton (1803–65). Hutton had five sons, three of whom joined the family firm, which by 1863 had a showroom in London in addition to the factory in Sheffield.

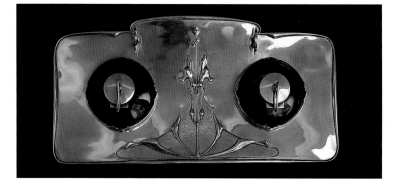

INKSTAND

DATE 1902
___

ASSAY TOWN London
___

MAKER William Comyns
___

HEIGHT 7.5cm (3in)
___

LENGTH 20cm (8in)
___

WIDTH 6.5cm (2½in)
___

Although it was made in London, this inkstand is in the form of a Napoleonic desk, even to the extent of the French symbols on the front.

William Comyns (c. 1837–1916) was apprenticed in 1849 to George John Richards of Clerkenwell, London, and he registered his first mark with Goldsmiths' Hall in 1859. About 1888 he took two of his three sons, Charles Harling (d. 1925) and Richard Henry (d. 1953), into partnership with him, changing the name of his firm to William Comyns & Sons.

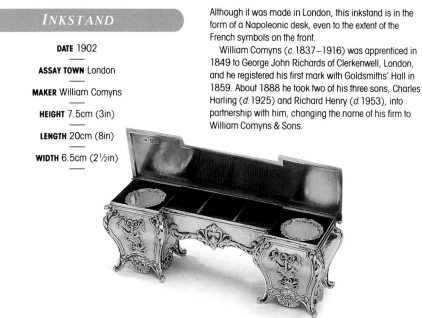

SHAVING BOWL AND JUG

DATE 1717

ASSAY TOWN London

MAKER Simon Pantin

HEIGHT (jug) 19cm (7½in)

LENGTH (bowl) 34cm (13½in)

This shaving bowl and jug were made by Simon Pantin (*fl. c.* 1694–1728), a member of a prominent family of Parisian goldsmiths and clockmakers and one of the numerous Huguenot craftsmen to flee to London after the revocation of the Edict of Nantes in 1685. He entered his mark at Goldsmiths' Hall in 1701 and set up his own workshop in St Martin's Lane, London, at the Sign of the Peacock; his mark shows a peacock spreading its tail over the initials *PA*. Much of his work is plain, only slightly decorated with engraving, and it is noted for its elegant proportions. His son, also Simon, succeeded to the business in 1731 but died in 1733.

Silver shaving bowls or shaving basins were known in the late 15th century, but the earliest surviving examples are from the late 17th century, although they are extremely rare. They were either circular or oval, as here, with a flat brim, which might be one-third of the width of the central hollow. The crescent-shaped gap in the rim was to go around the neck of the gentleman being shaved by his valet or of the customer being shaved by the barber. They were usually very plain, with, perhaps, some simple moulding around the edge and the owner's armorials. The jugs accompanied shaving bowls in the early 16th century (and probably before then), but surviving examples date from the early 18th century.

DRESSING-TABLE MIRROR

DATE 1886

ASSAY TOWN London

MAKER William Comyns

HEIGHT 53cm (21in)

WIDTH 36cm (14¼in)

Mirrors with silver frames are not very common, and they were probably made to accompany complete dressing-table sets. This cast and pierced silver-mounted frame has a wooden back with an easel stand. The decoration is a complicated pattern of flowers, figures and vases, with a grotesque mask at the centre top.

TOILET SET

DATE 1894

ASSAY TOWN London

MAKER William Comyns

DIMENSIONS (case) 35 x 15cm (14 x 6in)

These rococo-style silver boxes and jars, together with the button hook, shoe horn and silver-backed hair brush and hand mirror, are in their original fitted case. Many travelling dressing cases made both before and after this contained glass jars with silver covers, as well as such necessary items as writing pads, manicure sets and sewing equipment.

Comyns were among the most prolific makers of dressing-table objects of all kinds, producing often profusely decorated trinket boxes and powder jars.

CLOCK

DATE 1912

ASSAY TOWN London

MAKER Omar Ramsden and Alwyn Carr

HEIGHT 9cm (3½in)

WIDTH 9cm (3½in) (at base)

DEPTH 6cm (2¼in)

Omar Ramsden (1873–1939), who began his career in a Sheffield silversmith's workshop, became friendly with a fellow-student, Alwyn Charles Ellison Carr (1872–1940), when he attended evening classes at the local art school from 1890. In 1896 both men won scholarships to the National Art Training School (now the Royal College of Art) in London, and in 1898 they set up in business together, with workshops in Chelsea, London, where they produced a variety of gold and silverware, ranging from small domestic articles to elaborate ceremonial pieces. It seems likely that Ramsden did little of the actual silversmithing work, which may have been carried out by Carr or by an assistant.

Both men were impressed by the skills of medieval goldsmiths, whose works were keenly sought after at this period. Although the style of their work echoes the ethos of the Arts & Crafts movement, there are often strong elements of art nouveau in the overall design and decoration. Some of their work does, in addition, look professionally made, which is not in keeping with the Arts & Crafts philosophy. In 1910 they registered the mark *RN & CR* within an oval.

GLOSSARY

A

Acanthus The motif, based on the decoration often seen in Greek architecture, came to be used in England in the early 16th century and was popular during the reign of Charles II (1660–85) around the bases of two-handled cups, beakers, tankards and so on. During the neoclassical period it became stiff and formal.

Anthemion A decoration, based on stylized honeysuckle flowers and leaves, that was originally derived from classical architecture and that became popular in neoclassical design.

Applied Wire, moulding or cast pieces, such as swags and garlands, made separately and soldered on to the main body of an article, either to ornament or strengthen the item, are known as applied decoration.

Assay The name for the compulsory process of testing the purity of metals is taken from the Old French *assai* (trial or examination). All silversmiths must register their marks and details with an assay office and submit all work for examination. If the pure silver content is as represented, the work is hallmarked (officially stamped); if it is not, the piece is confiscated and, in most cases, destroyed.

B

Baluster Decorative pillars or stems, of the kind found on candlesticks, wine cups and goblets, are known as balusters.

Beading or **bead moulding** A cast wire, shaped like a string of small, hemispherical beads, was usually used as a decorative addition to the borders of salvers, tea sets, sauceboats and so on from *c.*1760 to *c.*1820, although it is sometimes found in late 19th-century pieces.

Bright cut engraving In this kind of facet-cut engraving on silver (and on inserts of silver into Sheffield plate), which was popular towards the end of the 18th century, the line was bevelled so that light was reflected from its facets to give extra brightness.

Britannia metal This base alloy, not to be confused with Britannia standard silver (*q.v.*), is composed of 150 parts tin to 3 parts copper and 10 parts antimony and was often used as a base for electroplating from *c.*1840.

Britannia standard Between March 1697 and June 1720 a higher standard for wrought silver – 958 parts per thousand – was compulsory, and it was indicated by the figure of Britannia. The change in the standard of plate was intended to discourage its purchase and to stop silversmiths from melting down silver coins, which were of sterling quality, for their work. The use of Britannia standard became optional after 1720, and although it does not wear as well as sterling silver, it has continued to be used from time to time.

Burnishing The lustrous effect created on silver or other metals by the use of a hard, smooth tool made of agate has, from the early 1800s, been achieved by machine polishing. Burnishing is only occasionally undertaken these days.

C

Caddy Tea used to be sold in boxes containing slightly less than 1¼lb (550g), and the Malay word for that weight was *kati*, 75 *katis* equalling 100lb. In the late 18th century the word was transferred to the container.

Cartouche This tablet ornament, usually oval, with a decorative or scrolled edge, generally has a coat of arms, design or inscription in the centre.

Castwork Decorative or functional elements made in a mould and soldered on to an article are known as castwork.

Caudle-cup This two-handled vessel has a swelling, globular shape below, curving inwards at the centre and outwards to the rim, usually with a cover.

Chasing Relief decoration, often to form patterns of flowers, foliage and, sometimes, figures, was made with a hammer and punches of different shapes and sizes and did not involve any loss of metal.

Chased up Cast objects were finished by this chiselling technique.

Chinoiserie A form of decoration popular in Europe inspired by Chinese sources. It was introduced at the end of the 17th century and reached its height in the 18th century, coming to an end *c.*1795. The vogue was manifested in architecture, interior decoration, furniture, porcelain, tapestry, wallpaper and decorative objects of all kinds. It was superseded by Japonaiserie (*q.v.*).

Close-plate During the 18th century everyday objects – e.g., spurs, knife blades and buckles – were made by soldering a thin foil of silver onto iron or polished steel that had been dipped into tin. The piece was always burnished. More cost-effective methods rendered this process obsolete during the 19th century.

Cut-card work A form of decoration in which pierced silver plates, cut with a chisel into, mostly, leaf patterns, are soldered to the exterior of an object. The style was introduced to Britain from France in the mid-17th century and seems to have been practised by Huguenot craftsmen. It was used around handles of, for example, coffee pots to strengthen the joint. It is often used with beadwork stem decoration.

E

Egg and dart or **egg and tongue** This repeating border ornament, of classical origin, was used on plate from the renaissance onwards. It consists of rows of alternating ovoids and arrowheads.

Electroforming In this spin-off of electroplating metal is electro-deposited into a mould and removed when it is sufficiently thick to produce a freestanding object. The method allowed intricate items to be reproduced for a fraction of the cost of handmade items.

Electroplating This method of coating an object with silver by passing an electric current through the object and a solution of cyanide of potassium, which causes the silver ions to adhere to the object. The

process is sometimes used to conceal the discoloration caused by alterations to antique silver.

Embossing A type of chasing in which the metal is hammered and worked from the inside.

Engraving One of the best known decorative techniques in which the silver is removed in a series of lines of different depths to give the effect of shading. It was used for simple inscriptions and complex armorials and also for decorative work. Engraving was often not carried out by the silversmith but was sent out to a specialist.

F

Flatware The generic name for knives, forks and spoons.

Flute A long, vertical and rounded groove in a column.

G

Gadroon A type of decorative edging, often found on the edges of trays and the rims of goblets and so on, widely used in the 17th and 18th centuries and sometimes today on traditionally styled objects. It consists of a border of vertical, slanted or spiralled reeding (*q.v.*), usually done by repoussé (*q.v.*).

Gilding The application of a thin layer of gold to a metal surface.

H

Hollow-ware The generic name for items of household silver other than flatware (*q.v.*).

J

Japonaiserie After the opening of Japan to the west in 1854, Japanese-style motifs became popular in both the decorative arts and furniture.

K

Knop The protuberance in the

stem of a goblet or standing cup, or a knob, such as that forming the handle of a lid or cover (often in the form of a flower, acorn or pineapple).

L

Let-in shield Because it was not practicable to engrave Sheffield plate since the copper beneath would be exposed, a hole was cut in the object and a piece of solid silver or "shield" of metal was soldered into position for engraving.

M

Matted A flat, sunk background that is dotted with punch marks, created by a matting-punch, a burred or round-headed punch.

Medallion A circle or oval containing a decorative device, usually of classical origin – e.g., a head or figure of a goddess.

N

Neoclassical The style popular in the late 18th and early 19th centuries and characterized by columns, swags, ram's heads and so forth.

Niello An alloy of sulphur, lead, copper and silver was fused, powdered and pressed into lines engraved on silver, thus producing a decoration of black lines when the excess was polished away.

P

Parcel-gilt or **party-gilt** Only part of an article is covered with gilding – for example, a design in relief may be gilded to contrast with the silver background.

Patera (pl: **paterae**) Circular or oval relief ornamentation, usually with geometric rayed or leaf patterns.

Plate The word used before 1743

to describe articles of solid silver and gold. It derives from the Spanish word for silver, *plata*, and correctly describes all early solid silver. It is often mistakenly used to refer to fused or electroplate.

Porringer The name generally used in the United States for the one-handled vessel known in Britain as a bleeding bowl. In Britain porringers generally have two handles.

Q

Quadruple plate This US trade term suggests the number of times an object has been dipped in the plating vat during the plating process. It is one of the commonest plate thicknesses, and only federal plate is heavier.

R

Reeding A decoration formed from parallel convex ribs.

Repoussé The ancient art of raising ornament in low relief from the back of an object using punches and a hammer.

Rococo The style favoured in the early 18th century, which is typified by an asymmetrical use of scrolls, shells, flowers and foliage.

Rolled edge The edges of Sheffield or fused plate articles were rolled to conceal the copper centre, which would otherwise be visible. The silver was either folded into a rim or a narrow mount was fashioned and soldered to the edge.

S

Sheffield plate Two pieces of silver foil with a layer of copper sandwiched between are fused together and rolled into sheets or drawn into wire. The process, invented in 1743 by Thomas Boulsover (or Bolsover, 1704–88), provides a metal that can be worked like silver. Unfortunately, it was not especially durable and was complicated to make, and it was superseded by electroplating (*q.v.*). The manufacture of Sheffield plate was not confined to Sheffield.

Silver gilt The thin covering of gold over solid silver.

Spinning In this method of producing hollow-ware (*q.v.*) a flat sheet of silver is fashioned over a shaped wooden chuck fixed to a rotating lathe.

Stand Items such as teapots and coffee pots were sometimes made with complementary stands to protect table-tops from heat and water.

Standish An inkstand.

Sterling silver Metal consisting of 925 parts of pure silver to 75 parts of copper.

Strapwork Ornamentation of flat, interlacing bands was popular in the 17th and 18th centuries.

Swag A suspended festoon of foliage, flowers, fruit or drapery was a popular ornament among neoclassical silversmiths.

T

Tine The prong of a fork.

Tinning A cost-cutting process in the manufacture of Sheffield plate whereby tin is used instead of silver for the interior of, e.g., teapots or the underside of a tray.

Triple plate As the name implies, this is one thickness less than quadruple plate (*q.v.*) and as common.

V

Vermeil The French word for silver gilt.

W

White metal This hard alloy of copper and zinc is used as a base in electroplating.

Wriggle-work A zigzag or wavy line, or sometimes two such intertwined lines, was used to decorate borders.

– FURTHER READING –

Ash, Douglas, *Dictionary of British Antique Silver*, Pelham Books Ltd, London, 1972.

Banister, Judith, *An Introduction to Old English Silver*, Evans Brothers Ltd, London, 1965.

Belden, Gail and Snodin, Michael, *Spoons*, Pitman Publishing Ltd, London, 1976.

Blakemore, Kenneth, *Snuff Boxes*, Frederick Muller Ltd, London, 1976.

Fallon, John P., *Marks of London Goldsmiths and Silversmiths 1837–1914*, Barrie & Jenkins Ltd, London, 1992.

Inglis, Brand, *The Arthur Negus Guide to British Silver*, Hamlyn Publishing Group Ltd, London, 1980.

Langford, Joel, *Silver: A Practical Guide to Collecting Silverware and Identifying Hallmarks*, Apple Press, London, 1991.

Schwartz, Marvin D., *Collectors' Guide to Antique American Silver*, Robert Hale & Co., London, 1976.

Waldron, Peter, *Antique Silver: The Price Guide*, Antique Collectors' Club, Woodbridge, Surrey, 1992 (2nd edition).

ocupied ~ 1942-52
Japan

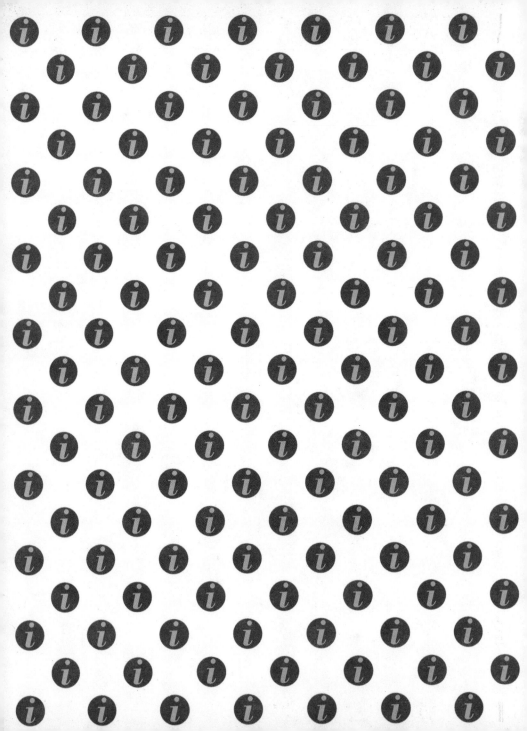